ne

our

ll th   t bel

Fr   rom th
01

019   01438
019   0143
019   0143

GRIZZLIES

IN THE
WILD

*Engraving of a Spirit Bear on the tomb of a Shaman/Chief,
Honnah Tribe, Southeast Alaska.*

GRIZZLIES
IN THE
WILD

WRITTEN AND PHOTOGRAPHED

BY

Kennan Ward

NORTHWORD
PRESS, INC
Minocqua, WI 54548

Dedication

To the thoughtful preservation of wilderness and wild animals, so that nature may continue to inspire people throughout the ages. To my parents Thomas and Elizabeth Ward, who gave me my first sightings in "the woods."

Copyright © 1994 by Kennan Ward

NorthWord Press, Inc.
P.O. Box 1360
Minocqua, WI 54548

Initial text and photography edit by Karen Ward

Designed by Wayne C. Parmley

Ward, Kennan.
    Grizzlies in the wild / Kennan Ward.
        p.   cm.
    ISBN 1-55971-425-5
    1. Grizzly bear. 2. Grizzly bear – Pictoral works. I. Title.
    QL 737.C27W37   1994
    599.74'446–dc20   94-20864

Printed and bound in Hong Kong

For a free catalog describing NorthWord's line of nature books and gifts, call 1-800-336-5666.

For more information on Kennan Ward stock photography and products, call 1-800-729-5302.

Table of Contents

Acknowledgments

A tremendous thanks goes to Thomas Bentley for text editing, also, to Larry Aumiller, Shane Moore, Walt Kiernan, and the staff at Kennan Ward Photography.

The last ten years have brought together many friends. Their companionship and support has helped not only in producing this book, but with the rigors of wilderness life. A special thanks to Helen Hamner for her countless help.

Many spirited people have lent a hand over the years to assist in planning our field work. They have supported our inspiration and our passion for photographing and learning about nature and have given us the reinforcement to thrive in the business realm. Thanks goes to: Robert and Carolyn Buchanan, Charles Mauzy, Lybby Moore, Ray Pfortner, Samantha Purr, David Rhode, Betty Ward, and Walter and Candace Ward. For continued support, our heartfelt thanks to Larry, Barbara, Kathy, Jim, Mary, Ellen, Paul Frear and their families. A very special thanks goes to the enduring spirit of Helen Rhode, 1919–1992, for being a source of continuing inspiration.

I am grateful to the staff at Kennan Ward Photography and to all the loyal customers who have supported our line of products over the last twelve years. Your support has helped us be a voice in wilderness preservation and education and has enabled us to work in the wilderness for an extended time.

With great appreciation,

Kennan Ward   Karen Ward

Foreword

KENNAN WARD first appeared in my office in 1978 when I was starting my teaching career at the University of California, Santa Cruz. It soon became apparent that what he really wanted to study was the "charismatic megavertebrate" otherwise known as the bear. Now, I like bears. They remind me of friendly family members. Unfortunately, I do not remind them of friends or family members. So my relationship with them has always been quite distant. Kennan, however, already knew a lot about bears and about Alaska, where he had been working. So, over the next two years I attempted to broaden Kennan's interest to include at least natural history and ecology and to bring him to pay attention to bear habitat—meaning the environment. In return, he taught me much about bears, culminating with his senior thesis.

After Kennan graduated he went to work for the National Park Service and later for the California Department of Parks and Recreation. In this later phase I met him again one mid-winter, in a cold, driving rain through which we hiked out to see the elephant seals at Año Nuevo State Reserve. His enthusiasm for wildlife and nature has always overridden any "minor" discomforts he might feel from rain, snow, sleet, or sub-zero temperatures. Hence, he can tolerate any-degree freezing weather in order to get just the right photo of the aurora borealis (which he has done) or other phenomena.

While Kennan was still a student he gave me one of his early photographs of a brown bear, which decorated my office for many years. I did not realize at the time that he was destined to become a really great nature photographer. But now his photographs speak for themselves, as you will see in this book.

What is most admirable about Kennan's work is that he avoids the cheap shots and "nature faking." He goes into the wilderness and seeks out animals not conditioned by frequent encounters with humans. His interest in animal behavior and ecology is keen and now goes well beyond bears. He is not content to take a picture and go away. He seeks to understand the creatures that he photographs and to comprehend what it is that they sense in their environment. This can be dangerous work, but he knows that. The rewards for such dangers you can judge, for they are here in the pages of this book.

Raymond F. Dasmann
Professor emeritus, University of California — Santa Cruz

Introduction

Bear country is a wilderness. The rugged, remote, and uncivilized landscape of a last frontier. Bears are part of the mountains, the valleys, and the streams. We refer to our landscapes with the names "Bear Mountain," "Bear Valley," and the hundreds of "Bear Creeks" (57 Bear Creeks in Alaska alone)—these names are used even in areas no longer inhabited by these monarchs of the animal kingdom. The largest land carnivore, bears once roamed a majority of the world's temperate zones. Today, south of Canada only remnant populations exist, mostly in large national parks. For us to truly survive with bears we must enter their world and understand their path.

Bear country is a smell. The scent of mountains, of a salmon stream, of tundra, and of the ocean. Bears have all the senses of other animals and humans, but they truly believe only their noses. The common human expression, "I must see it with my own eyes," can be juxtaposed with the bear's, "I must smell it with my own nose." A bear can smell farther than we can see. They can smell beyond their visual reach and beneath the ground; they have the instincts produced by thousands of years of relying on their noses.

Bear country is a sound. Not a cry of the wild, for bears don't howl—they growl, but not very often. The sounds of bear country are the sounds that bears listen to: the quiet sounds of wilderness. The wind, a stream, the birds and other animals in play or alarm. The loud, wild sounds of a large roaring river, or an avalanche, or a lightning storm, or an earthquake that builds the mountains or cracks them to pieces.

Bears show no fear of the wilderness—they are as comfortable there as we our in our living rooms. This may be their single most attractive and interesting attribute to humans. From ancient times to the present, we have looked upon these virile animals' strengths and have communicated about them among ourselves in symbols and metaphors. As people, we have been afraid of the wilderness, so we have "civilized" it to fit our needs. The bears have mastered survival in the wilderness and are a vestige of our lost connection to the land. The free, uninhibited ramblings of a bear can only be found where man is not (or does not exercise his privilege to be) the top predator—where man respects nature and her flora and fauna.

The bear is both the symbol and the living embodiment of wilderness. It can stand on two feet like a human, and it eats some of our favorite wild foods (salmon and berries), yet it is stronger and more adapted to the rigors of the wild than we are, so we envy it. The bear is widely represented in human culture, from the lighthearted play of the teddy bear to the supposed medicinal properties of bear gall bladders. The bear is a barometer of the survival of our own wilderness ethics and our own instincts.

The bear is a gauge of the health of the wilderness. The diversity of wildlife in the wilderness is the standard for a healthy environment, a standard established long before human encroachment. The preservation of that diversity is the reminder and the challenge of our changing environmental ethics.

Like some fish stories, bear tales run as far as the imagination will go, often with exaggerations and embellishments. Enthusiasm and fear drive these tales. With understanding comes knowledge, fact, and

increased respect. My photos are the "from my eyes" truth of my stories, which show that nature is at times unbelievable. What is presented here is a documentary of my times spent with bears over the last fifteen years. Here are a few of the stories and pictures I have caught. What is missing are the "ones that got away." Those are the incidents and intrigues that keep me going back to photograph. What is presented here is only a small portion of what was actually observed, and for technical photographic reasons, missed.

Those technical miscues were sometimes due to fogged lenses, or frozen batteries, heavy rain and snow, or the unrelenting attack of mosquitoes and flies. Even the photographer's folly of being out of film has stopped me, as well as having been the victim of cameras that failed for no obvious reason. On more than one occasion, simple fear, the avoidance of a possible face-to-face bear encounter, has caused me to sacrifice a photographic chance.

These photographs are the truths of my life. The wild animals and scenic wilderness landscapes presented here are shown exactly as nature presented them. Join Karen, my wife and fellow traveler, and me on an exploration into the wild lands—and lives—of bears.

Bear Woods

from the Eyes of a Child to the Lens of a Man

WHEN I WAS FIVE YEARS OLD I would tag along with my four older brothers and sisters in the wonderful deciduous forests of northern Illinois. (We simply called it "the woods.") I was afraid of the woods, and I know that my brothers and sisters were too, but they were bigger than me, so they never let it show. As children we imagined a bear lurked there; often when we heard a sound we would run in delighted terror, in one case fleeing from a rummaging pig! Development took the woods: an interstate to the west, tract homes to the east. All that remained was a vacant lot on our side of the construction.

The new houses brought more people, and the differences they brought made me begin to miss that fear of the woods. I missed its solitude and the power it held over my imagination. My feelings of that time changed my life. My memories still pivot back sharply to our summer retreats into Wisconsin and Michigan to visit my mother's 10 older siblings. My favorite and deepest memories are of "Shell's" (named after the Shellhammer family), a neighbor's several hundred-acre retreat with an eighty-acre lake. Adjacent to Lake Michigan, this land was a true bear woods. I remember seeing tracks of bear, deer, raccoon, rabbit, and other small mammals. For me this was heaven, and today its vividness remains deeply meshed with my recollections of my early family life long since passed. Seldom is there a family reunion without talk of the woods or Shell's.

One summer night at Shell's I sat up in bed, and soon I was in tears. My father thought I had a nightmare, but I hadn't started crying until long after I woke. I was too young to understand my emotional flare-up back then, but I think it was prompted by earlier talk about leaving in a few days for the summer. That triggered the memory of coming home from the prior summer to the loss of our woods. I recognize the face of my sadness now, because I feel the same each time I leave a bear wood. Maybe it's the beauty of untamed nature that I miss, or that the laws of nature feel so comfortable. Maybe it's having to face the problems of too many people and their pain in place of the sweet mysteries in the fear of the woods.

Once on a family fishing trip deep into the bear woods we spotted a female black bear. We all spread out to get a better look, but soon the rest of my family returned to fiddling with the fishing gear and digging into our food cache. I followed the bear for a distance and witnessed the moment when she caught up to her two cubs. I stood frozen as I observed the mother bear lie down to allow the bawling cubs to begin nursing. I watched until I heard calls from my family that meant I was in trouble. Even then I stood a moment longer in defiance. Returning to our camp, I told them what I had witnessed, but being the youngest, my story was deemed unlikely. However, that first observation (relived many years later when I photographed a sow grizzly with two cubs nursing) shaped an early interest that remained strong enough to become the focus of my college work and park service career, and later on my primary photographic theme.

Fishing had the attraction of bringing me close to nature. Catching night crawlers in the dark after a rain was my favorite task. Every morning and evening I would search for the fattest, longest worms. We fished in lakes, and if the worm was heavy it would go down deep where the big fish were.

Being out during the filtered light of dusk and dawn provided opportunities for observing nature: lightning bugs, frogs, and snakes all had their intrigues, and I often captured them for temporary pets. Getting up early to catch fish was even better than dreaming about it in bed. Many times, poles in hand, we saw deer, owls, songbirds, and lots of animals and insects.

I would become restless after catching a few fish, but if we didn't catch anything I would remain so quiet that it was almost a state of meditation. I perceived that if you didn't catch fish it was considered somehow "wrong." But after a couple of bass or northern pike or a lost musky story filled the morning, I would ask to get dropped on shore to escape the rocking boat. My walks along the lake would drive the bass out toward the boat at the edge of the lily pads. This "chore" allowed me to look for frogs, snakes, and animal tracks. Bears would come down to drink water, and every so often I'd spot a huge exaggerated track that would separate the grass and mud.

Being outside, my extra energy was not as noticeable—I would go all day exploring and learning about my home range. I probably to this day draw a better mental picture of Shell's than of my true childhood home.

After high school I worked as a seasonal employee for the park service in California at Big Basin Redwoods State Park. The job helped me in many ways: it covered my university expenses, it provided inexpensive park housing, and it kept me in a wild setting where I could learn more from the wilderness. The University of California at Santa Cruz was thirty miles away. I signed up under renowned wildlife biologist Ray Dasmann in the natural history program. Ray helped stimulate interest in habitat management, which enlivened my course work in biology and zoology. I continued with my position at Big Basin for six winters while I worked my way through school.

Summers were altogether different—two summers I worked with the National Park Service as a backcountry bear-management ranger at Glacier National Park in Montana, where I gathered information that went into my university thesis, "The Co-evolution of Bears and Man." I spent one summer rangering in Redwood National Park on the northern California border. Another was spent in Denali National Park in Alaska. After graduation I worked in Yosemite National Park, Sequoia National Park and at Año Nuevo State Reserve with elephant seals. Twelve years ago I returned to bears, my most photographed subject, and the source of a constantly renewed attraction and satisfaction.

Is That a Grizzly

behind that Elephant Seal?

IN THE LAST YEARS of my ranger career, I was assigned to Año Nuevo State Reserve in California. This picturesque spot is where elephant seals come each winter to breed, give birth, raise their young, molt, and to rest on shore where they fast for up to three months. The position I held was classified as a "permanent intermittent" job, which allowed me to work in naturalist activities three months out of the year and freed me up to work on photography for the remainder. I tried to split my focus between the two careers over the different months of the year, but I found it was not possible to do both jobs well. After a few years, photography became a full-time vocation. While working as a ranger I was exposed to all sorts of camera crews, still photographers, and writers, each with various interests, styles, temperaments and funding. What I perceived to be missing was the educational approach, that of supplementing photographs with informational text. That is when I discovered my niche.

Año Nuevo State Reserve includes Año Nuevo Island and a seven mile stretch of California coastline. In my naturalist duties at Año Nuevo I would pause at the cliffs above the beach with a tour group of up to 20 visitors and describe a scene from hundreds of years ago when Sir Francis Drake anchored his boats just offshore on New Year's Day. What is today Año Nuevo Island was then a point of land, Punto Año Nuevo, Point of the New Year.

From searches with long spyglasses aboard the boat, Drake's men spotted a beached whale. Hearing the news, Drake sent two boats filled with 20 men each to shore. With their single-shot muskets in hand, the men landed. Not understanding if the whale posed a threat to them, nor indeed what the beached whale truly was, they were alarmed when the enormous creature began to move! Quickly the men lined up in combat file, the front row of men on one knee holding their shooting position, while the back row of men stood just behind them with muskets ready. Thinking the whale was still alive, the men fired 40 rounds into it and began to reload. If they had not been in such a hurry to come ashore they might have noticed that they were not the only ones leaving footprints on the beach. After the barrage of shots, several large California brown bears, or grizzlies, came out of the whale carcass. (The terms "grizzly" and "brown bear" are often used interchangeably. In North America, the name "grizzly" is applied over much of the animal's range, though "brown bear" is used on the coast of southern Alaska and nearby islands, where the animals are much larger than those inland.) The men were not fully reloaded when the bears, unaccustomed to humans, dispersed. According to Drake's journal, one bear was killed while inside the whale carcass.

I would then point out to my tour group at Año Nuevo the Waddell drainage and talk about the salmon that spawned in that watershed. The salmon and abundant foods washed ashore by the mighty Pacific Ocean, combined with the warm, plentiful California winters, kept bears in this region fed year-round and produced very large bears. In fact, California was a great habitat for brown bears—and still is today for the California black bear.

Perhaps not an altogether great habitat: roast grizzly steaks were a specialty in the restaurants of mining and railroad camps in California. Bear fat was used as oil, and hides made great rugs and bedding.

Brown bears had survived for thousands of years in California, but the local population was decimated during the period of 1849–1870.

On October 5, 1875 lumber baron William Waddell was killed by one of the last grizzlies surviving in the state. By 1886 no bears existed on the central coast of California. By the early 1900s, the state had lost the largest population of brown bears known in the world. Today, a grizzly appears on the state flag and other official state emblems including the California State Parks shoulder patch worn by all rangers, a reminder of a grand animal we can no longer see in California.

This history on the decimation of the California grizzly provides a sharp warning: in a few short years a thriving population was wiped out. Today in Alaska, 1,300 bears are killed annually. But this legal, regulated killing of bears, although an ethical problem to some, will not eradicate bears, as long as the human will exists to save the species. This will didn't exist in California during the 1800s. These days, habitat loss appears to be the more serious menace.

Often someone in the tour group would tire of my bear obsession and say with annoyed enthusiasm, "What about elephant seals?" I would respond that elephant seals never came ashore on the mainland when grizzly bears patrolled the beaches. Elephant seals returned to Año Nuevo Island when bear numbers dropped. In the last 20 years, elephant seals have moved onto the beaches of the mainland.

Elephant seals spend almost their entire lives at sea, coming ashore in the late spring or summer for a couple of weeks to molt. The males stay ashore for up to three months to breed. Females come ashore for two weeks in spring to molt and for a month in winter to give birth and wean pups. After weaning their pups, the females will breed and return to the ocean.

Though they are no longer predator and prey in California, seals and bears have a similar biological trait. Bears eat clay and vegetation causing a tar-like fecal plug to form prior to hibernation. This winter fast of hibernation or "denning" is similar to the physiological changes an elephant seal goes through while on shore. After the elephant seals left their breeding grounds, I would often find tar-like fecal plugs, similar to those of bears. Bear plugs hold body warmth and stop the stomach processes while the bear hibernates. Elephant seals do not eat or drink for the period that they are ashore, and for them, the fecal plug preserves moisture during their exposure to the sun, wind, and weather.

As a naturalist, I find that comparison and observation are the best form of natural history education and communication. Bears have always fascinated us, filling our history and culture. More than any other animal except the primate, bears are very much like us. Bear mothers have long nurturing bonds with their offspring. Bears stand bi-pedal, eat the wild foods we too favor, and live in the lands we most value as wilderness.

Bears have many of the virtues and vital activities of human champions. And even as I patrolled the shores for elephant seals, bears were on my mind.

Look for a Tree!

(a Ranger's Lament)

THE PARK SERVICE HONED MY SKILLS and interests and gave me an opportunity to observe bears. Bear management is an interesting concept—in private I always referred to it as "people management." Bears were hard to "manage." To illustrate: High up on a rock along Mount Grinnel in Glacier National Park, I rested from an early morning trail patrol. I watched mountain goats feed and golden eagles soar. A grizzly bear had been seen near the Grinnel Glacier trail and I wanted to keep an eye out in case of trouble. After scanning with binoculars up and down the trail, I heard some growling and branch-snapping. I scrambled along the rocks to a cliff.

Just below were two bears fighting. Small trees snapped as the fight went on for half an hour, then suddenly one bear dropped flat, prone on the ground, and the other moved on top and they began mating. This was the first time I had observed anything like this. It was amazing because the aggressor had been the female. I theorized that she wanted to test the male's strength and endurance prior to mating. They remained coupled for most of an hour as I watched from my perch. My radio had been turned down so as not to startle the bears, but it was now time to check in.

I was informed that a bear had treed a group along a trail on the next ridge over. If I cut across country I could cover the distance in two miles, otherwise it would be a four-mile trip via the trail. Toting my 40-pound rescue pack, I went across country and arrived to find a young (often dubbed a "hooligan") bear tearing into a day-pack. Four people decorated the subalpine fir trees. I asked the people if they had seen any other bears in the region, but no others had been spotted. I was hoping the young bear did not have a nearby mother, although from its size it appeared large enough to have been weaned. I spoke loudly and firmly to the bear. I picked up a rotten log and threw it down on the ground halfway to the bear, creating a strong ground vibration. The reluctant bear moved up the trail towards the mountains. I helped the people out of the trees and sent them back to the trailhead, then proceeded farther up the trail in case more people were in need of assistance. What a job!

From a clearing I was able to see another small group of people a half-mile up the trail. Calling loudly, I was able to warn them of the approaching bear. The bear left the trail and moved into the thick woods. The group of hikers joined me as I directed them toward the trailhead. Suddenly, out of the forest, the bear moved toward us in a false charge. My official job description called upon me to protect people and property and preserve the natural resources for future generations. For a moment I stood "protecting" people from harm, pointing a .44 magnum pistol at a bear who was 15 feet away. What a mess. I spoke firmly to the bear, advising it to move on. I stared down at my hand on the gun. What seemed like an hour was probably no more than a minute. The bear was wise and slowly backed off and retreated up a ridge.

Members of the group, grateful for my help, wrote letters on my behalf, and at the end of the year I was presented with an award of achievement by the National Park Service. To these people I was a hero, but I felt alienated and had a strange sense of dislocation. It had seemed very inappropriate for me to be in this bear's territory, with artificial power over its life.

In another bear encounter (this one on my day off), two other rangers and I were forced by a bluff-charging bear into an old wooden boat. We avoided more complicated problems by shoving the boat out into the water. As the bear started to follow us we paddled away furiously with our hands. There we were, the district ranger, a backcountry ranger, and the bear-management ranger, escaping a grizzly bear in a leaky boat without oars. The bear patrolled the shoreline neck-deep in the water, displaying its profile while popping its jaws in threat. We named this unmarked bear Josephine Red because this contact happened on the north end of Lake Josephine in Many Glacier district. Josephine had the reddest fur of any bear I've seen to this day. We had to modify the name to Joe Red, however, when we observed the bear standing.

We wound up drifting for about an hour in the boat, so we discussed bear strategies while radioing back to headquarters for some oars. Since it was my day off, I was carrying a day-pack and camera. I took some identification snapshots of the bear to illustrate my thesis work on morphological characteristics. This snapshot (from 1978) was published and used by the National Park Service for slide presentations and bear information.

Many bears in Glacier National Park are familiar with humans, and these people-habituated grizzlies may know they can harm us and that we often cannot retaliate. Young bears, like people, test the limits in their environments. The most common defense for anyone in a grizzly encounter is to climb a tree, if trees are available. (In high tundra areas, you have to stand your ground and make loud noises). In fact whenever I walk a trail, I always examine trees for their climbability. For this purpose, the best trees have alternating lower branches for steps and a perch 20 feet off the ground that would be comfortable for one or two hours.

Look for big trees with long large branches made for overnight perches or high overlooks for spotting bears. Sleeping in one of these would guarantee you a safe—but long—night.

Bears move around in Glacier National Park in response to food availability and denning needs, according to the season. One of my thesis investigations was with avalanche chutes. I was trying to predict bear-use areas based on food availability, investigating habitats that had been changed due to avalanche or fire or other disturbances. Avalanche chutes are the path a snow mass takes as it slides off a hillside—a mighty power that can severely disrupt an area of trees, vegetation, rocks, and possibly a winter den. This clearing of the tree canopy and brush allows light to reach the ground the next summer, changing a climax forest into a newly exposed region of primary plant development. It would take many years before a true forest zone would begin again. However, in just three years many foods preferred by bears are found growing in these avalanche chutes.

I studied three areas where in 1975, 1976, and 1977 avalanches had cleared trees and brush close to a trail or backcountry camp. These snow chutes had disturbed the area enough to return it to being a community of seral (young) vegetation. Over the next three years, bears were attracted to the tuberous plants that grew there. By the summer of 1978, bears were digging regularly in these areas, sometimes creating confrontations with people. The idea of my study was to identify which habitats would attract bears and predict bear activity, thus allowing bears and people to go about their needs in mutual peace.

Well, the implementation of a warning system was not so easy. Though huckleberry patches, like the avalanche slopes, were known feeding grounds, it was not readily accepted that bear feeding habitats and seasonal movements could be predicted. Year after year, however, rangers would be faced with "the day of the grizzly" (which seemed to occur around the first of August), when the fields of huckleberries brought berry pickers, both human and bear, into conflict. The huckleberry patches are thick and brushy, and it can be difficult to tell if a bear or person is nearby. The bears quickly learned they could approach and frighten a person away from a morning's berry-picking and make off with all the berries. Now these known patches are closed in August until the bears have consumed most of the berries.

Complicating these encounters was the difference between the people I would talk with in the backcountry and those in the "front country." The front-country visitors were self-assured, sometimes angry about trail closures and protective of their rights and tax dollars at work. In the backcountry, hikers wanted to be informed of any bear sightings and were concerned about bear behavior and interested in their natural history. They also wanted an understanding of their place in the wilderness alongside the bears. They came into the wilderness to experience nature and to learn more about themselves.

Time in bear country will teach you that camping requires careful planning, proper food storage and preparation away from your sleeping area, and sensitivity towards low-impact wilderness practices. It is an enjoyable experience if you come prepared, and a potentially hazardous one for both bears and humans if you don't.

Bears Own Our Dreams

LIVING AND WORKING IN BEAR COUNTRY certainly entails a change in lifestyle. I enjoy tent camping, the fresh air, the sounds of nature, and the firmness of the ground beneath my sleeping bag. There is something powerful and restorative about sleeping out in the bush and being a part of nature. When sleeping in a house, my dreams are far less frequent and vivid compared to my dreams outdoors, even in non-bear country. Tent camping is like joining a new community. Most animals adjust to human neighbors, but some bears seem to come around only when things are still and quiet.

During the night bears have an advantage. Relying on senses other than vision, bears' sensory readings in the dark are very accurate. Food is available at night, trails can be managed by touch, and bears seem unaffected by the elements, something I have deeply admired about wildlife.

Bears own the night—and sometimes the dreams—of tent campers. Resting in bear country half-awake, I always have more fear for Karen's safety than my own. I picture my father-in-law saying, "I *told* you not to camp in bear country with Karen." If I were injured in a bear attack, I would accept it as a hazard of my job, but I feel responsible for bringing her close to danger. In wild areas I will only rest after an active patrol through the dusk. I always drink several jugs of water before bedtime to force myself to get up during the night to check the area or put more wood on the fire.

Once, this state of half-sleeping, half-waking went on for a couple weeks on Shuyak Island, located on the northern tip of the Kodiak Archipelago, Alaska. I was so sleep-deprived I had difficulty making sense. One night early in the expedition we camped in a lovely cove. The water was glass-calm as we landed our small inflatable skiff, which was filled to the brim with gear. We set up camp while watching the alpine glow paint Mount Illiamna many miles away. We knew we were in bear country, so we made a large fire. So large, it took both of us to haul another log on from the abundance of driftwood that encircled the cove. There were no signs of recent or frequent camping. The high number of eagles, bear, deer, sea otters, harbor seals, and other wildlife confirmed that the cove was a sanctuary. Seven loons chorused in the twilight very close to our camp. We called the unnamed bay Seven Loon Cove after their inspiring song. With a sense of unparalleled awe, we retired to our tent as the fire roared.

Sometime in the middle of the night, Karen woke to the crunchy sound of footfalls on the stony beach. I was half-awake when I too heard the rhythmical crackle of moving gravel. In a flurry we gathered the flashlight and signal horn and exited the tent. Listening, we were able to distinguish two sets of steps approaching along the edge of the water. Blasting a loud air-horn designed for signal use on a boat, we broadcasted our position. The echo resounded throughout the cove, followed by silence. I waited for some moments and upon hearing the footsteps once again, repeated the air horn. Before the echo returned we heard footsteps running toward the forest and away from our beach camp.

Knowing the behavior of bears, I told Karen that if they wanted to traverse this corridor, they would probably soon return. As we discussed strategy and loaded up our smoldering fire, Karen elected to stay by the fire for the first watch. Firelight illuminated the waterline and the forest.

We gathered rocks, sticks, the boat motor (to safeguard it), and anything we thought might scare off unwelcome visitors. Dreams of bears getting to Karen woke me every half-hour with an automatic, "How's it going out there?" Soon her two-hour shift was over and it was my turn. An owl hooted in the forest of Sitka spruce. A hare nibbled on beach grass. The harbor seal in the cove inhaled and exhaled as he crossed the water. Seven Loon Cove was especially quiet and calm and acoustically wonderful for broadcasting the sounds of nature.

As darkness waned to dawn a sea otter splashed as it dove beneath the water. An eagle called out as if a rooster of the wilderness greeting the day. Songbirds trilled a chorus to the dawn while perched like ornaments on a Christmas spruce tree. The morning mist from the bay dampened wildflowers and our camp. Morning is slow in this north country, as it starts only a couple hours after the sun sets. Sunset is after 11 P.M. and sunup is just before 4 A.M., with twilight lasting throughout most of the night.

Walking around camp in the growing light, I gathered firewood and cameras and set out along the beach. Karen rested after her night watch. I looked along the way for tracks but the morning-dew-covered rocks gave me no clues. I took a couple landscape and close-up photographs. I walked around half seeking photographs and half looking for signs that would explain last night's visitation. Soon I found fresh tracks, two sets, leading away from our beach camp. They were dug deep into the thin layer of soil that braided together the forest edge, where the grassy meadow transitioned into the beach gravel.

When I returned to camp, Karen and I laughed when I told her that we'd spent the night protecting ourselves from a couple of (ferocious) deer. The locals would have called us "*chechakos*," or green-horns for our nighttime antics.

A few nights of half-awake sleeping later—each taking two-hour watches inside the tent listening for any disturbances—we woke in the morning to find seven large scats close to camp. When the bears did visit us in the night we missed the sounds completely.

Not so Neighborly
on the North Slope

ABOVE THE NORTH SLOPE of the Brooks Range in northeast Alaska lies the flat coastal plains of the Arctic National Wildlife Refuge, commonly called ANWR (pronounced "an-warr"). In the United States, this is one of the last large wilderness regions remaining relatively pristine. Until recently, when oil exploration moved more people onto the North Slope, this area was comparatively unvisited by people outside of the native coastal communities.

There are no roads here. To get to ANWR you must fly or catch the one annual boat that services the villages. To fly there in a Cessna 185 from Fairbanks takes between two and one-half to three hours, depending on weather. There is no fuel outside of Deadhorse, Arctic Village, or Fort Yukon, which is at least an hour's flying time away from ANWR. The pilot must plan ahead for his fuel needs by making early fuel-storage runs whereby he carries 15- and 55-gallon plastic fuel tanks up to the north slope and stashes them at his personal landing and refueling rest stop. Without these fuel caches, the return trips wouldn't be possible.

Caribou in this region congregate during specific times, such as birthing and also when they gather and move in a group for insect avoidance. From the air, a hundred thousand caribou can be seen condensed in a tightly knit group, closer than even the wildebeest migration in Africa. Smart predators follow this migration and learn the timing of prey behaviors.

Caribou tend to birth in traditional areas. We have camped along their route hoping to photograph this magnificent wildlife drama. From the air we would pick out campsites ahead of the migration, guessing which direction it might move. If the landing site was new to the pilot, several passes would have to be made to get the feel of the land to see if a landing was possible. Hazards for the small plane include rocks, bumps, and other landing-site ground conditions. Pilots need to know if the ground is dry or boggy and how much flat space is available for takeoff and turn-around. They must also judge wind direction, reliability, and speed.

On one excursion, after a few passes over one river bar landing, our pilot spotted his opening. He bounced along on the large tundra tires of his Cessna 185 tail-dragger on the makeshift runway. He leaned out his window reviewing the rocky river bar and said, "It's going to take some work to take off from here with a load." It was late May and the snow and ice were just starting to melt. We unloaded several weeks worth of gear and asked him to check up on us over aviation radio and advise us when he would be back in the area. He said he had a river float-trip charter the following week and would fly by. We cleared several rocks from our makeshift runway to smooth it out, and following the roar of takeoff, we watched the small plane pass through an opening in the clouds, listening as the rhythmical engine sounds were replaced by the hum of silence.

As we debated which location to choose for our ten-day campsite, we weighed the probability of daily changes in the snow and ice, the river heights, wildlife trails, and the availability of drinking water. We found a spot of higher ground near a branch of the river, and we moved our gear off the gravel bar.

The unevenness of the land, its propensity for bogs and marshes, and the state of constant change make travel difficult. Walking the seemingly open tundra is a task. A strong hiker equipped with

hip-boots in an average bog-tussock area may cover only one mile per hour. Pingos—mounds of tundra and ice that form when water, trapped by the permafrost, freezes and expands—dot the landscape and can in extreme cases reach one hundred feet high.

As we began to set up our gear, Karen suddenly cried "Wolf!" Goose bumps accompanied our sense of defensiveness. She abandoned camp set-up and instead readied cameras and tripods. Five wolves traveled downstream toward our camp, fanning out and trotting directly toward us. Karen named the approaching group "Young Jaws." We must have landed along their travel route. From a distance they surveyed us and our camp. A large 100-pound wolf approached, raised the fur on its neck ruff and snarled. The pack fanned out more, and one came up from the far side of the surging river, while the others went up upon a snowy mound and off along the western horizon. That moment is sealed in Karen's and my memories, a time when awe was freely mixed with apprehension.

The wolves patrolled the area irregularly, as we did, waiting for the caribou. Evenings, from dusk through dawn, were the most rewarding. Adventures unfolded while the midnight sun never slipped below the horizon. We would head out on a hike around nine P.M. and return at four or five A.M. One foggy evening we decided to follow a trail of wolf tracks up the river. Several miles away from camp we climbed a hill and scanned the coastal plain and the route upstream. About two miles from us, farther up on a ridge, we spotted a bear. This grizzly was feeding on a snow-free, wind-blown grassy patch. New vegetation surely occupied its immediate concentration.

Alarmed, we strategized about safety, routes, and protecting our camp, with its two weeks' worth of provisions sitting in a rock pile nearby. The bear

could easily cover the ground to our present location and to our camp. But we had work to do, so we set up long lenses and prepared for a photograph. The warm light bathed the Brooks Range for hours as a drama unfolded within this dreamscape.

We were not the only ones watching this approaching bear. The wolves had moved into the opening a mile to the east of the bear, and we caught sight of them. One after another they slowly stepped out of the brush along the river bank—seven of them. The wolves were upwind of the bear, and the wind brought no knowledge of their presence.

Behind two adult wolves were four small brown pups. I assumed the adult pair were the parents protecting their offspring, although they could have been other caretakers. The pair moved 50 feet then lay down to wait for the pups to catch up. The adults repeated their movements, leading the young away, leaving a lone adult to confront the bear. Still unaware of the wolves, the bear finished grazing the small patch of new-growth vegetation.

Suddenly, the lone adult wolf charged directly at the bear. The bear stood its ground and then charged back. With quick reflexes, the wolf maneuvered to the bear's side. For 20 minutes the wolf and bear were locked in fierce confrontation, the wolf biting the bear's rump as the bear turned. The distraction allowed the pups and two adults to move along a ridge parallel to the river. In a stand off, the attacking wolf stood howl-barking at the bear, changed positions, and repeated its piercing bark.

The bear and wolf conflict demonstrated the elemental strengths of both predators. The wolf's fast reactions were matched by the bear's endurance. When the pack was clear of harm, the wolf no longer needed to protect the area. The bear seemed to ultimately win out, as it was not deterred from its original direction of travel. It continued up the embankment while the lone attack wolf watched quietly nearby. The bear finished his search and roamed the braided river to the east, eventually traveling up the far ridge away from the river.

In their search for food, bears travel corridors that intersect the caribou migration, searches which also may turn up eggs of ground nesters including Brant's geese, tundra swans, snowy owls, jaegers, and other terns. In order to increase their odds of finding food, interior bears (grizzlies) travel long distances. This enlarged home range intersects that of many other bears as well. Occasionally bears find themselves in the middle of a caribou aggregation. A hunting bear will endlessly pursue the group of

caribou ahead of it. With great endurance, the bear waits for a mistake or a slow, weak, or young animal. The wolf, on the other hand, generally picks out a weak individual before moving in. With calculated energy, wolves move toward a specific kill.

Bears pursue caribou on the North Slope more often than bears do in other habitats, particularly because there are fewer nutritional plants in the shorter growing season in the far north, and because there is such a high number of caribou. The caribou young provide easy targets, and there are also more old, weak, or sick individuals in this large population. In spite of the odds being with the bears, however, they don't succeed in many of the kills they attempt.

The tundra at times appears so sparse that it seems as if nothing is there. At the other extreme, the unending migration of caribou makes it look as though the ground itself is moving. During the midnight sun predator meets predator, and the strategies of survival are put to the test. The Young Jaws wolves returned with the pups that same night. After getting settled, a couple headed off on a patrol, two went in the direction the bear had gone, and two headed toward us.

One of them, a large whitish, tawny wolf, gave a haunting howl followed by a rapid bark when it discovered us. We called it "the white hyena" for its odd howl. This wolf stayed 150 yards away patrolling a 180 degree route around us. As we watched him the temperature of the night rapidly fell 10 degrees, bringing the chill to near freezing. A moist coolness stole over the land, hinting of the possibility of snow. It could have been the influence of the winds off the Arctic Ocean fifteen miles away. At 7 A.M. we decided to return to camp. A long night filled with memories to last a lifetime, and yet no worthwhile photographs came of this evening's encounter.

A photo shoot with captive wolves might have provided a quantity of sellable photos—more than I was able to obtain in this location—but I doubt that the story of that kind of an encounter would be as memorable or exciting as the experiences gathered on this long, cold, midnight sun-lit evening and morning on top of the world.

Wolves and bears have more run-ins than you might think—certainly more than I thought. One spring when Karen and I were photographing the glacier bear (the rare blue-phase coloration of the American black bear, *Ursus americanus*), we came upon an unusual sight near the mouth of a stream that emptied into a brackish tidal lake. We found the nearly perfect skeleton of a small black bear, complete with the skull intact. There were also some older remains in the same area, but at the time we were distracted by having this opportunity to photograph the rare blue bear of Glacier Bay National Park, Alaska.

The bears come to the edge of the ocean shore, to sloughs and to tidally influenced lakes to feed on sedges as they begin to sprout. During the early spring, sprouting sedges have a much higher percentage of crude, concentrated protein than they have as mature plants. This nose and appetite for protein that the bears possess help them build body strength quickly as they emerge from months of entropy during hibernation.

Coastal bears (whether brown or black) and interior bears all respond to the seasonally abundant protein in sprouting plants. Coastal bears change from a sedge diet to a diet of salmon when the protein content of the new plants drops. Thomas Bledsoe in his book *Brown Bear Summer* (Penguin, 1990) studied the content of protein during the summer at McNeil River, Alaska, and found a correlation between the reduction in crude protein and the timing of the beginning of fishing behavior.

Knowing that bears need this precisely timed food source of grasses, sedges, or fish has helped me find bears to photograph. Here in Glacier Bay National Park, a wolf with strong instincts also demonstrated an ability to predict bear activity seasonally. We had been photographing the blue and black phases of the black bear for several days along the tidal lake where we found the skeletal remains. The days prior we had seen bears feeding in the same location, (which also helped us to discover the bones).

One day we saw a large, lone blackish colored wolf at the mouth of the inlet stream. The wolf had a

fresh kill. As we observed from a distance, we thought he had taken down a moose calf. I approached as silently as possible through the woods. Upon reaching a vantage point, I saw the wolf was picking up the carcass and dragging it in the direction of the woods. Then the carcass was identifiable—it was not a moose, it was an adult black bear!

The wolf had eaten the majority of this bear already, leaving the hide and bones neatly cleaned, similar to the other skeletons we had observed in this area from the years past. Later in the day when the wolf left for the trees with a bulging stomach, we read the signs of the kill written along the bank of the brackish lake. Unfolding before us were tracks in the mud—these showed the trail of a running bear chased by a wolf. A stream bisected their chase. On the far side of the stream, skid marks appeared—as if fur was being dragged along. Through the soft

mudflat on the far side of the stream and up onto a grassy peninsula was a trail of deep wolf tracks paralleled by the skid marks from the dragged bear carcass. A blood trail lead from the stream to the grassy peninsula, and beyond was the carcass. The throat of the bear had been cut open by the jaws of the wolf.

We summarized that the wolf had given chase toward the mud, then bit into the bear's neck as the bear got bogged down in the mud mid-stream. From the other skeletons in this area it appears this had been done before. I had never seen, nor could have imagined, a lone wolf taking a coastal black bear that weighed possibly 250 to 300 pounds. A pack of wolves, yes. This was a clear example of predatory instincts and learned behavior, particularly in light of the use of the mudflats as a tool to trap the bigger and stronger bear. You can bet when I return to photograph bears feeding on early sedges and grasses that I will use *my* newly learned behavior to watch for the wolf near those mudflats.

When Man
Meets Beast

AT THE TOP OF THE BEAR DOMINANCE hierarchy is a mature mother with two-year-old cubs. These cubs are well over half the mother's weight and maybe three-quarters of her size. The dominance of these mother-and-cub teams is invariably superior to other creatures they may face in the bear world. The caution of the mother and the curiosities of the young bears can present a danger to a single bear. Bears are solitary by nature, and when they come across a mature sow and her two or three large cubs, it can likely mean trouble.

In descending order (with some exceptions) the dominance hierarchy follows: first, sows with large cubs; then mature males (mature males [boars] will normally defer to females with cubs); sows with young cubs; mature pregnant females; mature females; subadult partnerships; then hooligans (just weaned bears); and lastly, unattended cubs. Not surprisingly, the lowest ranking individuals on the dominance hierarchy have the highest mortality rates. Following cubs, hooligans or solitary, immature three- to five-year-old bears have the next highest mortality. This may be primarily due to losing the initial guardianship of their mothers and also to the early defensive requirements of establishing a home territory or range.

When brown bear mothers have had their cubs for two or three years, a variety of weaning behaviors can occur. One autumn, we observed a sow with large three-year-old cubs lead her family 30 miles away from her home range. Once she was over several mountain ranges, she attacked her cubs in an unforgiving and repeated pattern. The cubs protested, probably expecting a new lesson in their development, but the one they received was the shock of their first instruction about weaning. One cub tried to follow and was attacked again.

After this additional lesson, the bewildered cubs didn't move when the sow quickly left the area in a different direction. I'm sure the mother, if not pregnant from a spring mating, was headed to a den site near the edge of her home range. The sow moved out of sight 10 miles away, and the cubs, recovering from the shock, remained in the new region for a few days. They then proceeded to travel the thirty miles back to the berry-feeding area they had recently shared with their mother, just as the first snow began to fall. (Autumn weaning is an unusual circumstance.) The next lesson for the weaned cubs would be how to den on their own.

Bears are as different from one another as are humans. Some are shy, others curious; no two are alike. Some newly weaned cubs approach other bears as if they were looking for their mother; other young bears stay clear of everything. Bears communicate with each other in many ways and have worked out strategies to minimize confrontation. Bears will present themselves to one another with a side or profile view, communicating dominance with a display of their size. Growls, jaw-popping, standing, and ground-pounding are all threats. The highest level of threat is a charge, which can lead to contact and can be fatal to a bear or any other animal.

Bears who are less tolerant of humans may be less tolerant of other bears. When Karen and I go into bear country, we observe the bears and learn which ones should be avoided and which could

be cooperative for photographing. Only after knowing individual bears, sometimes two generations of them, do we learn when we can cautiously approach.

On one trip to the Alaska Peninsula, we camped with bear biologist John Hechtel and cinematographers Shane and Lybby Moore. The Moores were spending their honeymoon miles from nowhere working on a nature television program including bears. Winter was closing in and 25 or so brown bears were in the area.

We had identified a nervous sow with a yearling cub. This particular cub had an overly curious side to him. He would repeatedly run up to other bears, looking to playfully surprise them. I wondered if he was crazy or if he had recently lost his cub-mate and was seeking out new play partners. Nonetheless, the unpleasantly surprised bear would bluff-charge the yearling cub to warn it away, and the cub would then predictably bawl with fright, alarming its mother into protective action. The mother would come running in a full charge. When approached by the charging sow, the challenged bear would first stand its ground, then charge back.

For the weeks we were there, we frequently observed this same situation, until it was our turn. In a wooded area we regrettably met "Missus Cottonmouth" (named because she was always foaming white at the mouth, a sign of stress). From a distance of several hundred feet she came directly at us. We were caught by surprise, even though we had been cautiously watching ahead and calling out to announce our path. I began to retreat, but finding nowhere to escape, I pushed Karen behind me. Remembering the lessons of the other bears who held their ground against the mother's earlier actions, we stretched our large raincoats up over our heads to make us look bigger, gave a deep call combined with a heavy stomp on the ground, and stood our place. The sow locked her limbs into a skid, and when she was 10 feet away, she turned at a 45 degree angle and sped off.

For a few moments all that either of us could do was stay put, our eyes wide and our breathing hard. The ground seemed like it was still ringing from her heavy, fast footsteps. It's been confirmed that a pudgy running bear can move as fast as a sleek racehorse. Karen couldn't get the detail out of her mind that a single golden birch leaf had stuck to the fur of the sow's flank, and with all that tremendous speed and motion that leaf had remained as if glued in place.

Shane and Lybby were up on a nearby hill and heard our yelling. Right afterwards they observed the sow and cub tearing across the meadow beneath them, moving on out of sight. Shane's comment was, "Did you have to scare her that much?" I replied, "I don't know." I had never rehearsed this situation before and didn't have my lines down pat. Back at camp, John Hechtel gently scolded us for our encounter, following up his reprimand with, "That should have happened to me—I've been working with bears for the last 10 years and now you go and get an experience I haven't had yet!" That broke the tension of the encounter and we all laughed.

We were grateful we hadn't been "jawed and pawed." We examined the skid marks from the sow's front paws and found eight feet of disturbed ground. We were lucky this time, because our communication worked. If this had been my first day on field location and I didn't know how the other bears had treated this sow, we might have been in a difficult position. I study bears' behavior, both body postures and vocalizations to categorize their dominance and relationship to one another. Only when a recognizable bear is identified do I consider a respectful, informed approach.

Close Encounters: How a Bear Thinks

Bears in inhabited areas of parks or reserves deserve full caution and respect. There was a bear in Glacier National Park that would follow people in a determined manner when they were alone or in pairs, never letting up until they climbed a tree or got up high on a rock or cliff, or in water up over their heads. The only time this bear could be confidently dealt with was when a group of four or more people gathered—then the bear would feel outnumbered and leave the area. Meeting any unknown bear in the woods can be hazardous. You don't know what it may have just left: maybe a fight with another bear, or maybe it has a sprained paw or some bad berries in its stomach. Any number of factors could set the stage for its reaction to your presence.

Bears use trails as routes through their home range (an area including their den and seasonal food sources), to cross over into other bear ranges for mating or territory changes. Bears travel to food sources or day beds as part of their daily cycle. The home ranges of different bears can overlap.

Humans in a bear's territory most often take on the role of the traveling bear, unknowingly moving into the "personal space" of a bear. This territory may include a salmon fishing spot, a food source such as a carcass or berry patch, or a territory being "policed" by a sow as protection for her cubs. It's impossible for us to respond to a bear's challenge with a bear's strength or battle guile, therefore we must use all means available to avoid a close encounter.

To determine if bears are using an area, you can try using all your senses, including your olfactory sense: even a bear out of water has more odor than you might think. Also, be attuned to the sounds of nature around you.

Food or garbage smells attract bears. Body soaps, colognes, and scented lotions pique their interest. Bears' acute sense of smell is matched by their curiosity. Through adaptation, these characteristics have evolved bears into opportunistic omnivores successful in many habitats, able to enjoy a varied diet consisting of seasonally abundant food. Their exploratory curiosity sometimes brings them close to people. Squirrels have the same curiosities as bears, they will approach us, stand up, sniff around for food, and finding it, consume the offering. Equating food with humans, a squirrel will come running when it hears humans. The squirrel's behavior and that of a bear are quite similar.

This is a good reason why food and wild animals do not mix. Leaving scraps out means you can never be sure what you might attract. Even small animals have problems adjusting to human foods and their sudden loss of availability; after a season of learning dependence upon people, they sometimes starve when people leave. Feeding wild animals eventually results in wildlife encounters. Squirrels will often become a nuisance and persist in begging long after the food is gone. They may chew their way into buildings after the people leave. Ravens learn how to tear apart backpacks in search of food, raccoons get into everything, bears cause costly damage. Human foods generally are not good for wildlife. Animals are healthier eating the foods they find on their own in nature.

Bears generally keep their distance from large groups of people. In most public bear-viewing areas, people stay in predictable areas and defend their "territory" by repeated visits. In some bear habitats, including those with bear viewing in wildlife refuges, national parks or reserves, many bears have become habituated to humans. The bears that don't habituate stay away or use areas at night when the human activity is low. At distant locations within the same park lands, bears that are not used to humans may run at the first sound or scent of a human a quarter of a mile away.

When photographing bears, use a long lens. In order to successfully photograph bears in remote areas, it has been necessary for me to utilize a combination of techniques, the most important of which has been time.

Our admiration for and desire to observe bears is not usually reciprocated by bears. Bears tolerate humans in order to take advantage of abundant sources of food. Consider those areas humans visit to see bears: McNeil River, Brooks Falls, and the Denali National Park road corridor in Alaska. Bear activity in these places is different from the behavior of bears in the Arctic National Wildlife Refuge or other areas beyond the frequent exploration by humans. Bears' behavior in remote areas resembles the demeanor of any truly wild animal—avoidance if given the opportunity. It is always preferable to avoid conflict by preventative means.

Bear defense

When in bear country stay alert, listen to other wildlife cues, and, if possible, keep the wind at your back announcing your scent to the bears ahead. Talk loudly when in visual range, stay in a group. If you are alone and you see a bear, climb a tree beyond the bear's reach—20 feet to be safe — or climb up on a rock or cliff or move to higher ground. Move slowly but persistently. Step off trails, and give the right of way; sometimes bears just want to move on by.

If your visibility is limited in brushy areas, make noise, clap your hands, bang on things. If backpacking, pack food in airtight, and if possible, bear-proof containers. Don't carry fragrant foods or eat where you cannot clearly watch for a bear's approach. A campfire, where and when permitted, sends out the signal "humans are here." Smoke from your campfire also scents your clothes with a recognizable odor.

If a bear approaches, don't run. Anyone running from a predatory animal is inviting a chase. It could prove fatal to try to outrun a bear. Lift your arms with your jacket flared up over your head to make yourself appear larger and stand on a rock or log. In the event of a charge, road flares can be effective: the sound of the sizzling flame, the smell of sulphur, and the flame itself all work to deter a bear. Flares, however, are not used by many land-management organizations, especially in fire hazard regions. Consult local administrative brochures, rangers or public safety officers. Bear spray works effectively, especially for curious younger bears. When I choose to carry bear spray I am very careful. This device may give people a false sense of security, especially when you consider how ineffective it is in open, windy conditions, when the spray can become harmful to the user.

Removing or loosening the safety can accidentally cause the spray to go off, as a close friend discovered when he accidentally sprayed my car radio when handling the can. The car windows were up, and we came rolling out of that car as quickly as possible. The potent red pepper has left a permanent scent and color on the radio. I have left it there to remind myself to be careful. Pepper spray is nasty if you find it working against you—use caution and be sure to caution your friends. When flying, always protectively store it in a hard plastic or metal container that seals tightly.

When Beast Meets Beast

The bear has reflexes and reactions comparable to any top carnivore. The Spanish who colonized California enjoyed the sport of bear fighting. They would bet on how many bulls a bear could kill as the bear was restrained by a tether. The "sport" tested the bears' strength against the world's strongest and largest mammals. Bears normally killed or held off several bulls before getting killed by a fresh bull.

When bears travel they are vulnerable to other bears. In traversing a corridor from a huckleberry, soapberry, or blueberry patch toward another berry patch, a lone bear silently walking along may run into a large boar or a sow with cubs, who may react by standing or snorting out short huffs. The traveling bear of medium age, weight, and disposition retreats slowly, at first looking back toward the other bear. If the other bear gives a charge, the startled bear will run away for a short distance with the speed of a quarterhorse at full gallop. If caught, the chased bear will turn, growl, and face its opponent.

When their appetites are at issue, bears can truly be formidable foes. Bears time their arrival at fish runs with zeal, craving this highly sought-after food even more after a month or so of eating mainly vegetation. Though the early sedges that make up a large part of the bears' diet after denning have concentrated levels of protein, salmon sharply spur their appetites. If an eagle is heard announcing the arrival of a run of fish to its mate, or loudly protecting its catch, a bear will come quickly. When the salmon are running, there is a subtle change in smell, both in the water itself and in the air around it. This scent is especially significant to the acute senses of the bear. The fish are very strong when they first arrive and the bears are out of practice, so there is a lot of running up and down the river as they give chase. Soon other bears arrive, and the normally unsociable behavior of the bears is tested.

Bears adjust to the close proximity of other bears and work out their hierarchy as each becomes satisfied that they will get a plentiful supply of fish. Although some fights occur, they are rarely fatal. Fights with sows that have small cubs to protect prove to be the most physically harmful. Major injuries are also inflicted when large boars fight during the mating season or when bears are competing for winter-killed carcasses or for other early food concentrations. However, many bear "fights" are simply subadults or young adults sparring. The playful acts can go on for thirty minutes to an hour, often ending when interrupted by a mature bear, or another run of salmon.

Encounters vary in severity when bears seriously combat one another. Bears are built to withstand rough contact. Their fur and hide are thick and their muscle mass and overall size has earned them recognition as the largest land carnivore. (Polar bears utilize a mostly marine habitat and are classified as a marine mammal.) When two bears meet in battle, fatal injuries are rare, but occasionally scars from the wounds can be severe. When strength and size are unequal, most fights are over quickly. Seldom is a fight enduring unless the two are equally matched. Given a break in the fight, a less dominant bear will run or retreat quickly. In many instances sparring is a playful encounter of mature siblings, or a mated pair out of season.

Change of Season

(Cycles of Birth and Death)

DEPENDING ON THE LONGITUDE, the summertime extreme of the summer solstice can provide a day length between 18 and 24 hours. This keenly contrasts with the winter solstice schedule of between zero and six hours of sunlight per day. In the productive Alaskan summer season, abundantly rich food sources such as berries, fish, ground squirrels, and grasses flourish in response to the photo-period (change in the angle of the sun's rays and increased amount of daylight). Bears also respond to these seasonal foods (if they are lucky enough to locate the right ones) by reaching their maximum weight and ultimate physical condition.

By autumn this feeding bounty begins to dwindle. The cooling days and lengthening nights begin to slow the bears' metabolism. This is my favorite time to work with bears because they have beautiful coats and they experience the relaxation of full-stomach lethargy. As fall progresses, this sluggish state really takes over: after a night of rest comes an early-morning nap and a mid-morning nap and a late-morning nap and then some berry eating followed by an extended afternoon sleep. Depending on the air temperature, bears could sleep away 90 percent of the day, twitching and flinching like a dog in REM sleep. I wonder if they are remembering all the fish, berries, matings, or fights of the season.

As the bears begin to slow down, they also begin to move towards winter den sites within their home range. Bears use several methods to guide them to and from specific locations along their range. One such method employs their keen sense of smell. They rub themselves against trees and scent posts probably because it feels good, but this behavior scents the trees with hair and a recognizable smell. These trees may then be recognized by other bears as scent posts that mark the passage of the earlier bear. Several scent posts can be found in any region notifying bears following different trails what other bears are nearby.

During my university and summer ranger days I became intrigued with scent trees. Everywhere I went in bear country there were areas or rubs where bears—black, brown, or polar—left signs of their passing. My graduate thesis on bear behavior documents this activity around such trees and their increased use as bears moved from feeding areas to denning sites. Of course, I don't want to disregard the simple pleasure of rubbing an itch away, because the evidence is surely there that they enjoy scratching their backs. Seeing it in the wild awoke a memory of when I was young, watching my father, Thomas (an old bear himself), rubbing his back on a door frame.

Northern facing slopes or areas shaded during the winter months seem to be the favored den sites. Bears build dens sometime between September and October, typically when food-gathering tapers off following the first snow. Grizzlies will often build a snug bi-level den with the entrance below the bedding area to allow for thaw-draining and temperature control.

On their way to the site, they make several modifications to their behavior: rubbing on trees. They also scratch the ground looking for clay or condensed silt which they'll often eat—in some regions they also eat decaying leaves. They may get minerals and nutrition from these items, but they also eat them to stimulate the production of the fecal plug used to conserve essential body heat when denning.

Closer to the den site they become more secretive, roaming in circles as if searching or checking the region. Occasional digging is done as if to test the soil, followed by a flurry of digging as the actual den is started. Bears preparing to den may build one, two or three different "models" in similar locations within a radius of five miles. When it comes to bears and dens, no two bears are alike: some start a den, then return several times to finish. Some dig it, then go right inside, especially if it is snowing hard. Others dig a den, move a little bit away and dig another one, and then return to the first one to use it.

Pregnant sows are extremely secretive—they build their dens higher on the mountain slopes, deeper, and in colder areas. A pregnant female builds a nursery den that is slightly larger and often more carefully insulated with tree boughs, leaves, and grass, in readiness for the birth of the cubs during her winter sleep.

Grizzly bears are born in the den during January or early February. The young cubs are tiny and fragile. They weigh under one pound at birth. These undeveloped young—numbering from one to three (and rarely four)—instinctively suckle on their sleeping mother. After a couple of months of nursing in the den, they weigh between six and ten pounds when they trail their mother into a new world, emerging with her in springtime (typically in April depending on the climate and location). Being a mother of spring cubs is a demanding full-time concern. Having multiples of two or three cubs increases the demand upon the sow, and she must be very alert and wary in restricting their exposure to the many life-threatening hazards that lurk in spring cubs' new world.

Sows with cubs leave the den later in the spring than adult males (boars) and subadults (males and females), or adult females without cubs.

This ensures that they and their new cubs are not out when male bears are emerging from their dens searching for their first meal, when a small cub could be a menu possibility. The cubs are more mobile then, and food availability is better. This behavior reduces the chance of confrontation, especially in habitats with high "bear density." The very small cubs can be killed by other bears, golden eagles, wolves, and environmental hazards such as river crossings, cliffs, and vertical snow fields, in addition to whatever else young cubs' curiosities may lead them to explore. Strategic waiting prior to emerging from the den also ensures a better probability that the spring grasses will be up.

Occasionally in midwinter, if temperatures are warm (or the den becomes uninhabitable because of water or melted snow), bears may awaken and leave the den for a short period. Bears are sluggish when they wake, sometimes emerging from the den and stretching nearby for hours to reestablish bodily functions. Their fur is prime, full and thick, and rolling in the snow cleans and fluffs their coat. Any immediate wanderings could be hazardous: most grizzly dens are on steep ridges and coordination is essential before too much movement can be undertaken.

Bears mate in the early summer in May and June (and seemingly have a great time of it). A female in estrus travels to a springtime home range where seasonally abundant foods are located, areas that frequently overlap with the ranges of other bears. These "bear crossroads" are where the bears seek their mates. A male detects a female in estrus by smelling her pheromones in her urine. Typically unsociable, the boar breaks his solitary habits and follows the female. The pairing up of a bear couple can take several days; the female will travel around the overlapping ranges and may not mate until she is fully receptive. Fights sometimes occur if he presses her to mate before she is ready.

Other times all that is required is a great bear hug for mating to commence. The male locks his front limbs about the female's ribs, and the pair stays coupled for an average of 45 minutes. The male mates, then keeps a grip while he rests, then there is another coupling flurry followed by the maintenance of his grip while seemingly resting.

One time I observed a male who fell asleep between matings. When the female became conscious that she was supporting all that torpid weight, she turned her head and began biting the male. He responded by waking and once more copulating. Once this initial pairing is completed, there will often be a couple of days of the pair traveling together and additional matings. Along the coast I've seen a variety of patterns, probably because there are more bears in the areas to interact, which provokes multiple matings with other bears.

Brown/grizzly and black bears regularly look for new spring grass, or other young green sprouts. The tender sprouting plants contain a higher source of protein in their early growth stage, prior to the vascular-cellulose buildup needed for mature plant structure and stability during the summer. If the bears are lucky they may run across a winter-killed mammal, although that is the exception.

Bears fully utilize this early vegetative food source and graze like an ungulate—even their scat resembles a horse's during this time. This early spring feeding-season allows the females to improve their physical condition prior to pregnancy. The female bear has developed a biological mechanism that delays implantation of the fertilized egg (zygote). This undeveloped blastula remains in suspended growth in the fallopian tube until late summer, when nutrients in the body ensure its healthy development. When there is the abundant body fat of late summer, the blastula implants in the uterine wall and embryo growth begins.

Cubs follow their mothers from the den to glacial streams, where the new sprouts of equisetum, the oldest vascular plant, grow. Equisetum is commonly called *dinosaur food, horsetail fern,* or *scouring rush*. This plant is a favorite from the interior to the coast for black bears, brown bears, and interior grizzlies. The cubs mimic their mothers, first tasting then feeding on the new sprouts. The parental investment and cub mimicry ensures survival; the learning curve for spring cubs is dramatically steep, requiring up to three years to complete.

Being an opportunistic omnivore is no easy task. The cubs are always active, from the den to springtime feedings on vegetation sprouts, to sorties in salmon streams and berry patches, to chasing ground squirrels and searching for roots and tubers or angelica plants ("bear nip," we like to call this much

sought-after plant that resembles wild celery). The migration that the food search instigates will take the cubs over mountains, through valleys, across rivers, snow fields and glaciers, each step a demanding new experience.

Black bears, when confronted by known or unknown hazards, climb trees. Their short-curved claws enable them, especially as cubs, to hurry up trees and avoid conflict. The brown bear, on the other paw, has long claws, an evolution of the more open tundra, allowing for den-building, digging out ground squirrels, unearthing roots and tubers, and for digging clams. While great for digging, these claws don't allow brown bears to climb trees very well.

This has caused the evolutionary dichotomy between black and brown bear behavior. Brown bears have evolved to stand their ground protecting their "personal space" around them, instead of retreating up trees as do the black bears. Some brown bears, particularly mothers, take this a step further: because of the limited amount of food sources, she has to protect more than her personal territory. Therefore, she will threaten, bluff-charge or attack any threat to her. Cubs learn from the continuous flow of new experiences. Some grow up seeing humans, others grow up with no reference to humans. Some mothers with young rarely cross the range of another sow and cubs.

The protection of feeding areas may be the most significant environmental factor that contributes to the behavioral differences between the coastal bears and the interior bears. Coastal brown bears enjoy abundant food and may be seen in groups of up to 60 bears at productive salmon streams. Larry Aumiller, an 18-year veteran of bear biology and an Alaska Fish and Game custodian at the McNeil River Sanctuary, has observed a peak number of 67 bears at McNeil Falls at one time. (This was in July 1987, when Karen and I were there.) Larry may be the world's most dedicated bear-watcher. In areas such as the McNeil River, only favored fishing spots are defended and dominance prevails. If watched carefully, the human fishermen at Brooks River can be seen to exhibit the same behavior as the bears. Humans wait to fish a productive hole, and as soon as a fish is caught and the successful fisherman vacates his spot, another takes it.

One rainy summer's day, I took the advice of an old Alaskan: "If you don't like the weather for photographs, take a fishing pole with you and go fishing until it changes." The coastal stream of my choosing was choked with chum salmon, but I was after a Dolly Varden (char family). Bald eagles arrived finding salmon close to the surface in the tidally waning river. Their territorial calls alerted bears, and amidst a procession of eagles swooping down upon the exposed dorsal fins of the fish and gulls eating eagle-killed fish carcasses, the bears came down to join in. Responding to the bird cries and the thrashing sounds of fish piled upon fish that the salmon made in the shallow waters, the bears leaped in. Surrendering the fishing pole, I retreated to my cameras for a better catch. The weather was still gray and the bears were mostly young, lanky hooligans, which made for less than prime photographic conditions, so I resigned myself to observing.

Later, when the tide went slack and fishing was easiest, the subadult bears became alert and jumpy, standing, sniffing the air, and quickly departing. The behavioral change in these subadult bears alerted me to the approach of a more dominant bear. I became cautious. Retreating to higher ground, I watched a sow with two spring cubs patrolling the river bar, retrieving salmon along the water's edge.

On the other side of the river a sow with three yearling cubs approached a successful fishing spot. The two female bears arrived as if they had timed their fishing with the ebb and flow of the tide. They seemed to know when fishing was at its best. Karen and I no longer fish as we used to; now we aim to fish like the bears do, approaching at the right tide, along with the ebb and flow. Mother bears instruct more creatures than just their cubs.

I don't know if it was a scent in the air, or a sound of a bawling cub wanting some fish, but the two sows stood, growled, and "jaw-popped" within a few hundred feet of each other, signaling their mutual uneasiness. As two matriarchs of the dominance hierarchy, they declared their desire to approach the fishing grounds. It seemed as if a long time passed while they growled and jaw-popped at each other, with their cubs standing behind. As the sows charged into the water and closed in upon each other the disturbed fish thrashed into a wave of motion and a standing brawl between the females ensued. The yearling cub stood nearby and one of the other sow's spring cubs ran to the yearling and leapt into its arms. The larger yearling cub held the spring cub off the ground, and both watched as their mothers began chasing one another through the water.

For that moment the two unrelated cubs were united in fear as their mothers were united in conflict. The yearling cub might have had a sibling cub at one time, and they may have comforted each other during conflicts. Perhaps a memory of this behavior, provoked by the approach of the spring cub, brought the two together in a momentary protective embrace.

The mother of the yearling cub, dominant in the conflict, returned and upon seeing her cub with the strange spring cub, she moved to protect her young by killing the young intruder. The other spring cub of the twin pair had panicked and run off and was now separated from all it had known: its sibling and its mother. The vanquished mother returned after her aggressor had left the area and as the high tide was returning. The young mother patrolled the area, found her dead cub and probed around the body, finally leaving in search of her second cub. For the rest of the day the sow went up and down the water's edge searching a route the cub had taken, but now the high tide covered the cub's path. We last saw the cub high on a far ridge. This mother did find her cub late in the day, but then lost it in yet another unseen incident the following month. Death is an ever-present possibility for these youthful offspring.

It's impossible and perhaps foolhardy to try to predict and understand all bear behavior: whether it was the amazing concentration of fish that provoked the sows' excitation or just the protective behavior of the mothers with cubs is hard to say. Perhaps the mothers had a previous encounter that exacerbated this situation, as I've seen with other bear/human encounters. I am strikingly reminded again and again that these are indeed wild, magnificent animals.

Is It Lunch Yet?

(a Tale of Cooperative Clamming)

BEARS HAVE A KEEN INSTINCT when it comes to food. They are built to move across the land with ease, searching out any food source. They will eat grasses, flowers, roots, carrion, ground squirrels, fish, insects, soil—and the list goes on. As opportunistic omnivores they will consume, outside of man, one of the most varied food menus in the animal kingdom. Often we find bears when searching for our own wild foods. In bears, learned behaviors are inspired and strengthened by food rewards. Like many other predatory animals, bears have a good memory. For bears, it appears that the higher the fat content of the food source, the better their memory.

As my professor at the University of California, Santa Cruz, Ray Dasmann tolerated my persistent "bear-ology." Often we would meet, and with a bribe of coffee I could extract a theme for another paper on bears. Somehow during these tutorial visits we left biology for a moment and talked about photography. I'm sure Professor Dasmann thought I would never make it as a biologist, for my photographic distraction was strong.

Professor Dasmann gave me words that have followed me into the field, words as integral as the tools in my camera pack. He said, "If you want to understand the predators, learn about their prey." The last 15 years have been channeled and focused by this statement, giving me memories so strong that it is easy to lose myself in them. With only a limited exposure to formal philosophy, I revere this as an existential observation. It has helped me not just to look directly at the animal through the camera, but to understand its literal and figurative path. Knowing something about the bear's prey helps me to anticipate its movements, and knowing what the bear might do in advance allows my camera to connect at a precise moment. Often if you see something of photographic value (unless the event is a predictably repetitive behavior or action), it will be too late to capture it on film, for the point of interest will have passed. Using one's knowledge of behavior to determine the exact timing of a potential action photograph is one of the greatest challenges of wildlife photography.

When Karen and I chose bears as a subject for our concentrated work, we passed over the better known and more civilized bear-viewing areas that hosted guest cabins and restaurants, partly because it was beyond our limited budget, partly because these regions had been worked photographically so many times, and partly from our lack of research on the reservation system. We would switch from running our self-publishing "garage" enterprise one month, to conducting fieldwork in the wild, not truly understanding what we were going to do in the larger scheme of things. In the first year of working with brown bears we went to Kodiak. After all, who hasn't heard of the Kodiak brown bears, equal in size to the great polar bears of the Arctic?

Although recently we have photographed in the more popular bear-viewing areas, every year we build on the foundation of finding a new, seldom-visited area to explore, where a different food source—as Professor Dasmann suggested—may be located for study.

Clam Bake

Watching bears feed on grasses one spring on the Alaskan peninsula, I mentally traced their emergence from the den of late April or early May, pondering where they could have found food besides the grasses of June and the fish of July. What were they finding in May and early June that could re-supply their strength following the long period of winter dormancy? Occasionally a winter kill is chanced upon, but that lucky occurrence is not reliable enough for the many bears that traverse coastal Alaska. If a part of the reason that bears sleep in winter is due to the lack of food, then why don't they continue their slumber until late May or early June, when more ample foods can be found? There must be other more obscure sources of nourishing foods.

My curiosity was not satisfied. I continued my research, "talking bears" with bear biologists and other bear enthusiasts, and talking to people familiar with the area either as guides, bush pilots, or researchers. In due time, I learned about an old commercial clam settlement at Swikshak Bay on the Alaskan peninsula. I wondered if the settlement had sprung up after an early explorer observed bears digging clams along the bay. As I researched this area I learned that a film crew had attempted to find bears digging clams at the abandoned commercial clamming operation that rests along the shore of Swikshak Bay, but they had not been successful. I made plans for a two-week expedition the following year, hoping that my luck would be better.

Will Troyer, retired wildlife biologist, joined Karen and me for the expedition. I chartered a Beaver float-plane and filled it with enough survival supplies and rescue gear to last a month. Karen did her best to add as much gourmet food and fresh produce as possible. Will brought along the ultimate gourmet item, a clamming shovel. With a clear window in the weather we headed out for the hour-and-a-half flight. We searched for bear signs as we flew low over the glaciers, valleys, and snow-capped mountains. The early morning light mixed with the splendor of glacial ice that was slowly melting into the broad greening valleys below was breathtakingly beautiful. We picked out a bay near which we spotted bears feeding on an abundant grass flat. The bears were in a meadow of tall grass in a short coastal valley framed by a magnificent blue ice glacier.

While white-water waves were breaking on the beach, we quickly unloaded the mountain of supplies from the plane and bid our pilot Ken not to forget us. Soon the float-plane taxied off, chopping through the inlet waters and roaring in a display of slowly mounting power. It was

Karen Ward

amazing to see this big, graceful amphibious aircraft overcome the strong winds. We moved our gear above the high-tide line and walked around scouting in search of a camp spot. Since there was no sign of any previous camping here and there was a lack of dry flat ground, we looked for a site, protected from the south-easterly facing bay, that sported a good vantage point for spotting any approaching bears. On a ridge spiced with spruce trees we found a campsite. From our drop-off spot on the beach we ferried our gear back and forth, and an hour later we were ready to set up our tents, just as clouds darkened the sky and the winds sprang boldly up.

For the next two days it rained heavily and the winds blew down anything not secured. It was nearly impossible to photograph. We explored the area and walked on the endless beach.

Every day we were there we found glass balls on the beach. The balls had been used as floats by fishermen on their nets. Greenish colored, they ranged in size from a basketball on down to as small as a tennis ball. I'm not sure if it's a modern good-luck omen or just a symbol of a remote beach, but a glass ball amongst the seaweed at high tide truly has a romantic aspect. Today, these lovely glass floats have long since been abandoned in favor of durable and inexpensive plastic floats. Some fisher-men say its been over 20 years since they used the glass balls. Other reports indicate that some Asian fishing villages still use them. Either long at sea or migrating with the tides far from Asia, these glass balls carried history, endurance, and finally, seclusion, and obscurity to this beach.

Finding the first float of the day was a game that the three of us played in the rain while we traveled the long beaches and high-water driftwood piles. While we searched we found the tracks of a wolf who had also patrolled the edge of the high tide. We must have just missed him, as the tide was retreating and the wolf tracks narrowly paralleled the surf line. A different kind of beach-combing was on the mind of the wolf. Its tracks told a great story of investigation. Beginning with a seaweed pile that hosted many nose prints in the sand around a dead starfish, along up the beach to a dead bird, further along the beach to a fish skeleton, then back to the shoreline. As I was kneeling over the wolf tracks around the fish skeleton a red fox surprised me from behind during its patrol of the beach. We both were startled, but didn't move except for the initial muscle-tightening response of surprise. Then the curious fox began an approach/retreat survey of Karen, Will, and me.

The limited exposure to people made this fox an instant friend. We unburied a seaweed-covered dead bird for the fox and he intently investigated, choosing to follow us instead of making off with the food. Days later we saw him find the bird and retrieve it. We followed the fox's tracks two miles down the beach until they ended in a wood pile. Our attention on the fox was suddenly distracted when we sighted a bear, almost a mile out in the mudflats during low tide of the early morning. The bear was significantly exposed and following the retreating tide line. We would be too if we followed, but nevertheless we gave it a try. With the wind in our faces and our hip-boots on we traveled over the clam-loving mud. We moved very slowly until the bear turned or put its head in a hole—then we moved closer.

That first morning was a learning experience. As we approached, the tide retreated another quarter mile and the bear followed the newly uncovered clam habitat. The endlessly long beach now became an endlessly wide mudflat. As far as we could see the shoreline was missing! Pockets of remnant water in shallow basins remained. With its broad feet, the bear moved with relative ease. Our narrow feet weren't as useful. After hours of approaching the bear, we saw the water begin to return. Small waves from the ocean began seeping into the basins, filling them to four feet deep. Following the tide, the bear was able to better predict and handle the approaching water. Soon he was closer to shore than we and he caught our scent. As we stood still, he looked our way, stood, snorted, and ran for a short distance parallel to the beach, then stood again. The water was rising higher on our hip boots as the bear retreated at a gallop up into the grass flats above the driftwood piled on the high tide line of the berm on the beach.

It was wonderful to see the bears of the bay dig for clams even at a mile-and-a-half distance. We traveled back to the beach in a zig-zag pattern around basins of seawater using our tripod legs to measure the water's depth. On shore we sat on a log and spread our gear as we discussed the beautiful location, the change of weather, and the natural history of bears and their food sources. In this timeless setting, we felt as explorers might have hundreds of years ago when they came across animals and interesting foods.

Will dug into the sand with his hands imitating the bears digging for clams; later Karen found a

bucket in the driftwood piles and they tried to dig clams for the three of us. I found the bear tracks and followed them off the beach through the driftwood pile until I found six or seven bears in the grass flats two to three miles away, feeding like milk cows in the field near my childhood home. I sat on a log and watched with binoculars. As I removed the glasses from my eyes, the glacial landscape of blue ice and mountains unfolded from the fog. An avalanche thundered and the calls of seagulls resounded off the distant peaks. The morning began foggy and cold, and now with the clearing and sunshine I was warm and content in the wilderness with the bears.

Watching the bears a distance away, with fresh bear tracks beneath my own, I must have drifted into a daydream, for all I remember is waking and seeing a fox resting a couple of feet away from my own two feet. It appeared to be the same fox we had seen before, although I wasn't certain. It watched me as I reached slowly for my camera gear. I spotted Karen and Will spread out on the beach relaxing. I joined them and told them about the bear tracks and the fox, and then discovered that the fox had followed me, appearing from out of the grasses and logs. We snapped a few photos, and the fox moved off toward where I had been bear-watching. We stayed and talked about the clam hunt.

The story of clamming was again interrupted by the appearance of the fox, so we grabbed cameras and photographed it amongst the beach plants and driftwood. The fox moved off again and we followed because the flowering beach growth added to the photographic appeal. After a half-hour of trailing the fox, we watched it disappear beneath a log pile. We had retreated but a few steps when we heard the low pitch of a kit. The adult had summoned its young out of the den. One, two, three then finally four fine young foxes appeared.

We spent most of the midday watching and photographing as the kits paraded around us. Later, we began repacking our camera gear for the long hike back to camp, when another fox appeared with a baby sea otter in its mouth to feed the pups. Cameras flew into action once again as the family of foxes investigated the next meal. The baby sea otter looked as if it had died and drifted ashore. Surprisingly, one of the adults dug a pit and dropped the sea otter into it and covered it with sand until it was completely buried, apparently caching it for a later time.

The foxes switched roles—off went the original fox down the beach on patrol as the new fox curled up and fell asleep along with the kits. We decided to check on camp and followed the fox tracks in the same direction. On the way home Karen found a glass ball and Will found an assortment of beach debris.

Some of the refuse looked Asian, some Russian and American. Buckets, fishing net, plywood signs, empty containers, boat bumpers—any imaginable floating garbage eventually arrives at the high-tide mark.

The next low tide was the following morning, so after lunch we patrolled the grass flats to make best use of the time. We quickly found a century trail, where years of bear tracks have formed deep repetitive impressions. We found ourselves walking as bears do—in a wide-stepping waddle. These trails had deeply worn saucer-sized impressions in the grass where the track made by the front paw was again stepped in by the rear foot. Probably, these trails have been used for centuries. They tell the tale of bear movements. These bears' instinct for spring foods indicates the same behavior bears have been locked into since the first bears inhabited this area after they crossed the Bering land bridge from Eurasia.

More is known about bear fishing behaviors than clamming behaviors. It seems that not enough of this behavior has been documented for it to be widely broadcast in scientific journals. The presence of abundant food influences the bears' movements. Extensive habitat is required in order for bears to acquire all the foods they need to prepare for hibernation.

Before dawn we decided to follow the tide out and approach a bear from a better starting point. Several bears had entered the beach a few miles north and were at the tide line following it out as we arrived.

We had hoped to intersect them somewhere before extreme low tide. We had a tide table that predicted the low tide. What did the bears use for tidal information? Was it instinct? Or was it a learned behavior, reinforced by the memory of high-fat food—timing the return morning after morning, perceptibly later each day. Yet the bears always showed up just at the right time, just as the low tide was stretching the beach into a perfect dinner table rich with clams—if you knew where and how to dig them out. Were the bears provoked by the sharp cry of seagulls or migratory birds hunting for exposed arthropods? Most likely it is the smell of the retreating tide or of newly exposed mud that attracts them. Nature has a way of communicating its changes through more than the visual sense-cue that we so rely upon. Sound, smell, and the gravitational pull of the moon contribute to the overall natural understanding of the bears.

With the ocean retreating a mile or so, the morning was calm and quiet. We could hear wasps flying across the mudflat. For some unexplained reason as we came closer to a bear, it changed from a patterned digging behavior to extreme jumping, running, rolling, growling, and bucking. We had never seen such an explosion before! Because more wasps were in the area we concluded the bear had been stung in a sensitive region, such as the nose. We saw this bear later rubbing its nose and repeatedly pressing it into the mud. After a short while, the bear went back to digging, but seemed to relapse again into a crazed fury. We quickly decided to back off from this situation and retreated before the tide to the upper beach.

A sow with tiny spring cubs was clamming farther down the beach, but the tide was bringing her back towards us. Even at one mile away, she was extremely intolerant of our presence, so we didn't attempt to move any closer. On the way back to camp Will found a glass ball the size of a softball but was less successful than the bears at getting any clams large enough to cook.

The late afternoon light brought Will and me out into the grass field over the "century trail" the bears had developed. All bears we had seen to this point had run, no matter how much distance was between us, once they realized we were nearby. This day we approached the bears feeding in the sedge with the wind at our faces. We used a sparsely forested spruce ridge to conceal our movements, and we set up our equipment among the last trees on the edge of the forest. From this natural blind, among the broom-handle-sized tree trunks we stayed until sunset and observed some unique behavior.

The grass field was about a mile wide and several miles long. Within view we counted 12 to 25 bears; at any given moment they melted from view when they stepped into a dip in the field—then they would appear suddenly when they climbed up on some driftwood or grazed atop a knoll. With their heads down in the tall swampy grass, the backs of these bears looked like cattle out to pasture. A large boar's feeding movements would influence all the other bears to move in relation to him as he picked a new area to graze. These movements brought the peripheral bears close to our natural photographic blind.

In late afternoon just before sunset, the bears' movement increased suddenly. Out of a hidden depression came a very large bear, relatively close to where we were watching from the spruce trees. Whether this bear had been sleeping in a hollow or had traveled along a meandering drainage creek lost to our sight in the deep grass was unknown. What I observed was the purposeful pursuit of another bear.

What appeared to be aggression turned into courtship. I was unable to photograph the first attempts of the bear's mounting because I was laughing so hard tears were rolling down my face. Will tried to quiet me so as not to alarm the bears close to him, for we were on opposite ends of a spruce patch with different vistas, keeping watch from both sides and behind. He had not seen the large bear, only the smaller bear in front of him. I was unable to communicate other than by pointing. Upon seeing the two bears his laughter echoed mine.

What was hilarious was that the huge boar had such a large protruding stomach that when he rose to mount the female his stomach pushed her forward and away. Finally, after repeated bumper-bear trials he nearly stood upright to fall down on her. Will and I photographed as they coupled for nearly an hour, with the setting sun painting the glacier and the grass flats with pink alpine glow.

The next day we were able to see many more bears as the tide began to withdraw and the sun began to rise. We followed the log berm behind the beach and approached the bears from a much closer distance. We watched and learned their technique: the bears would locate a pore in the beach mud, then with their front paws they would pounce with a down-and-forward motion onto the mud. This compacted the sand and silt mixture, keeping the digging clam from escaping. Slowly and cautiously the bear would dig, up to a foot or more deep, then gently lift out a delicate razorback clam with its paw. These clams, six to ten inches long, have a razor-thin shell and a long meaty foot. The bear would bite the tasty clam foot and with its claws carefully separate the clam's shell, often without breaking or destroying the fragile shell. I've never seen a bear so tender and precise. All that was left behind was a tiny muscle attachment on a dainty shell, which the waiting sea gulls would pounce upon. With my thumb and index finger I could easily damage these shells if I wasn't careful when handling them—how was it that a massive bear managed to leave them perfectly intact? Surprisingly enough, some bears could dig 40 to 60 clams or more depending on the length of the low tide.

Often there was a beautiful tale left in the wake of the feeding bears: a trail of big muddy footprints, a compressed region of the sand where the bear leaned down on one elbow while digging with the opposite paw, and a saucer-sized hole filled with water mirroring my curious face as I observed the scene. The dainty razorback clamshells, perhaps with some seagull tracks encircling them, seemed to softly cry out to be collected, not left to be taken by the tide.

Watching how bears compressed the mud and dug where they saw an air pore, Will and Karen hunted for clams in a similar fashion and were extremely successful. Clams were the highlight for our dinner. Another hunting skill we observed in the bears was their consciousness of the relationship of the waterline to the newly exposed beach. The most successful clamming occurred where the ocean had most recently exposed the mud. This explained why the bears moved in such a seemingly unpredictable manner: The tide did not retreat uniformly. There were many contours, depressions, and hollows.

After many days some bears seemed to expect us out there in the mudflat with them, as if we were other bears. As tolerance grew, both man and bear worked closer, and in time, without incident, I documented this unique feeding behavior. This encounter occurred after many years of dreams about this kind of natural cooperation and is the single most significant personal discovery I have enjoyed in my experiences with wild bears.

Could You Smile
for the Camera, Please?

I F YOU ARE INTERESTED IN SEEING BEARS, you will probably find your way to one of the few managed bear-viewing parks or reserves. Most photographers and bear enthusiasts enjoy the comforts of national park facilities and services. By volume, Brooks Camp in Katmai National Park and Denali National Park in Alaska have the highest records for the number of people per day who do see bears. McNeil State Game Sanctuary and Kodiak National Wildlife refuge have similar bear viewing, but limit the number of visitors allowed, which adds a level of quality and intimacy to the experience. We have made visits to these areas over the last seven years during different times of the season.

Most bears in these areas adjust to the presence of humans. Each refuge has many levels of bear-human interactions. Bears becoming accustomed to humans creates habituation that serves as a medium for peaceful coexistence. In these regions there are also less tolerant bears who are not habituated and come out only at night, or when humans are not as abundant, such as during rainstorms.

For bear photography these areas are the safest, but also the most photographed. I heard of one photographer at McNeil River who used 86 rolls of film in a single day. If you multiply an average film usage times the many thousands of visitors, the per-day photographic figures are astounding. On my visit to McNeil River sanctuary in 1987, Karen and I had one day of a stand-by slot. A National Geographic crew was there doing a television special on the bears. I cannot be sure if I reacted to the sound of camera shutters firing around me, or if it was the photographic possibilities of the sow that nursed 20 feet away, but I shot my record level of film in one day—28 rolls. There are only a few such magnificent wildlife shows on earth—no one comes away seeing or thinking about bears the same way afterwards. I have tried every year to win a lottery chance at the four-day permit and in eight years have managed to secure a single slot one time, which didn't leave room for Karen.

My interest in bears takes Karen and me into areas not often visited, partly because of access restrictions, but primarily because of our interest in nonhabituated bears. We also sought to view natural behavior less affected by the human presence—not the circumstantial running away from people that you find in regions where hunting occurs. Wilderness behavior in remote locations has occupied a large portion of our field time, but has resulted in only a small quantity of our total photographs.

I have grown to understand that nature is far more creative than I could ever strive to be. Wildlife and nature unfold their secrets to the watchful eye, in such a unique, often unpredictable way that cannot be created in captive or set-up situations. Many simply magnificent photos from the wild have been commercially imitated under controlled circumstances. This is a breach in the connection between nature and the original observer of that event. It is difficult for some viewers to understand the difference between photographs taken in the wild and those set up to imitate the wild. And it could be asked, Who cares anyway? The integrity of the photographer and the work is not readily understood.

Manipulated pictures made in a captive situation can give us a false sense of security that wildlife is in abundance, is easily accessed, and is waiting to let us approach it. The American style of photography leans towards portraiture: full-frame, close-up, anthropomorphic, "personality" photographs.

Other cultures that live in a more tightly condensed geographic region like to see some landscape around the wildlife, to show the wilderness aspect that belongs to the animal. I call this a "habitat photograph," as compared to the portrait image.

Bart is a large grizzly who is seen in almost every media presentation calling for a bear. He is available for on-location still photographs too. I love bears so much that meeting this bear would undoubtedly be wonderful. However, in order to save the authenticity of many months and years of remote fieldwork, through rain, loneliness, and unproductive down-time, I will refrain from photographing him. Maybe I could someday visit Bart, and leave my camera behind, for I know there is something to learn from him. My challenge, my wish, and my goal is a hope that with enough time in the field, nature will unfold its drama and secrets to a patient and attuned observer, who can recognize its ongoing marvels unfiltered by manipulation.

Common Ground

and the Higher Animal Spirit

ANIMALS HAVE LONG BEEN ASSOCIATED with guardian spirits in a metaphorical way, providing virtuous examples to emulate in our totems, ideas of reincarnation, and even our concept of god. I believe our regard for this "higher spirit" may actually come from the animals' continual relationship to instinct and man's continual loss of instinct.

It would be impossible to categorically identify a true instinct, for they remain one of the greatest mysteries of the natural world. We cannot always separate instinct from behavior that is learned. It is compelling to consider that animals, especially higher order animals such as the bear, live closer to their instincts yet have more open-ended behavior than the lower orders. Humans are increasingly searching for the answers that unfold this great mystery.

Bears have an irresistible urge to explore. This behavior helps them to find new sources of food for survival. This instinctive trait was woven with a long chain of learned behavior over the evolution of the species. Repeated behavior patterns may "become" an instinct after many thousands of years. A good example is the Asian bears who, during one of the ice ages, traveled across the Bering land bridge to enter a new, similar food niche in North America. While the advancing glaciers transformed the ocean's water into solid ice, the Bering Strait became a bridge of exposed land that allowed animals to travel and explore new lands and food sources. Prior to that, the bears had 100,000 years of continual occupation of the Siberian niche. Those bears who journeyed from the Siberian forests into the open coastal plains and tundra of North America evolved instinctual behaviors into new learned behavior. The first bears had a significant learning curve, with mixed results, though most of them were positive—based on the newly available food niche. Nonetheless, these bears had to react to the stress of a new environment much as we do when our world quickly changes. In broad terms, what were our comfortably repeatable behavior patterns yesterday are forced to become prototype learning behaviors today, based on the crush of new experiences, the immediacy of worldwide communication, and population stress. Similar to the bears who explore new lands, we sometimes find the changing world has little use for yesterday's instincts. However, old knowledge (instinctual and learned) can serve new surroundings in many species, especially generalists like bears and humans.

The generations of bears since the Pleistocene era have developed new, repeated behavior patterns during the last twenty thousand to thirty thousand years. During this "gestation" period the learned behavior has had the opportunity to become an instinct as part of the evolutionary process. This new set of instincts will have remnant Asiatic behavioral processes entwined with the newly formed evolutionary learned behavior. This behavioral mingling can produce "new" instincts over a period of time, perhaps from the first to last ice age.

What does all this have to do with higher spirits, you might ask? In a nutshell, this concept is a link to our own instincts. For me, the more I contact the natural world, the more I imagine (because I cannot precisely identify an instinct) my instincts to be working. The effect of that contact is balance, an overall well-being, bursts of creativity, patience, a prevailing feeling of contentedness.

This balance—that can be projected as getting in touch with our higher spirits—comes to each person differently, just as learned behavior has taught us differently. Humans and animals have two primary tutors, their parents and their mutual teacher: survival and experience.

Humans do not easily admit their animal ancestry, particularly the similarity of our reaction patterns that are consistent with many large mammals, such as primates and bears. The human hunter behaves much the same as other animals in that his survival often depends on analyzing the confrontation and intent of another species. With human or bear, these behaviors are parallel. The bear learns about man by collecting information from our scent trails. The best procedure for the bear is to circle back, because man tends to travel linearly; thus the bear reacts to avoid conflict. The reward for this skill is survival. A bear has nothing to gain in a man-bear encounter. In the last 10 years in Alaska over 12,000 brown bears have been legally killed by hunters, yet less than a half-dozen humans have been killed by bears.

The human hunter finds his learned behavior tested too, when mixed with new unexplored reactions to circumstances in the modern world. However, we should not have to kill an animal to come close to our instinct. When the first hunters turned into photographers and came back from field sessions with photographs instead of skulls and hides, I believe we came closer to understanding our relationships and common ground with animals. We know that we share some instincts and evolutionary paths with the beasts, but there is still a tremendous amount to be learned.

I am indebted to Roger A. Caras, author of *Monarch of Deadman Bay* (Boston: Little, Brown & Co., © 1969), whose work has influenced some of the ideas in this chapter.

Written with a
Wing and a Paw

(a Myth Message)

Bears possess great capacities for endurance, fearlessness, and flexibility. These qualities were not lost on the native people sharing their domain. To these people, bears were stronger than their most valiant warriors and as such, were honored much the same as a tribal elder, or "grandfather." The Native American term *peewa* means "grandfather," "respected one," and "bear." The bear is a prominent figure in Native American culture. A shaman, or medicine man with a bear as a totem or guiding spirit was seen as all-powerful. A shaman influenced by bear spirits would wear a hide, giving him the strength of the bear to fight off enemies or demons, to heal the sick or wounded, or to call upon the bear's enduring strength for the protection of his tribe.

Fear played a major role in influencing people settling throughout the bear's range. For the most part, these bear lands were located far away from settlements and were only traversed while hunting or traveling. Naturally as the bears wandered in search of food, they would occasionally use corridors that would intersect with populated areas. In those days, many tribes considered eating bear akin to cannibalism, hence bear hunting was limited to hide acquisition or self-defense. Often after a bear was sighted in the area, a rash of tales of encounters and incidents would ensue.

A balance of respect for and fear of bears ruled the thoughts and behaviors of the Native Americans. Here is a tale conjured from my own musings in bear country, which attempts to illustrate this balance:

While hunting, a brave came across signs of a bear. The hunter followed the bear's trail, because the hunter knew that bears observe efficient routes and utilize existing paths about which the hunter may not have been aware. Along the route, he saw evidence of the bear's digging for plants with fleshy roots and tubers. Mimicking the bear, the man tasted the sweet, starchy vegetation, and enjoying it, gathered some for his return home. Stepping over the bear's scat, the hunter recognized the remains of fish and realized that the bear had recently been feasting on a run of salmon.

Changing direction, the man traveled many miles to a favorite stream. He gave thanks to the father bear spirits for the gifts of roots and the dream of fish. Knowing and respecting the bear served this brave well, for by afternoon he discovered another bear in a shallow stream. Sitting on a nearby hill he paid respect to the fishing bear, giving thanks once again for the gifts the bear spirit had given him. The brave peacefully watched the bear go about its fishing. By not disturbing the bear, the brave learned new skills. As the brave watched the bear, he observed the bear's unique method of catching fish. The bear would chase a run of fish to the stream bank, swatting one out of the water and onto the bank with its paw. Thus the bear taught the brave not only where the fish were in the shallow area of the stream, but also the techniques for very successful fishing.

Watching the bear eat was another lesson in itself. The bear began by eating the roe, then the skin, then the head and lastly, the body. The brave decided

to try these other parts of the fish that he had been feeding to his dog. The man stacked a stone for every fish he saw the bear eat, not to tally up a score, but to mark the bear's power. The pile grew. As the bear ate, he left scraps that soon attracted an eagle. When the brave saw this, he knew he had been shown a special gift in witnessing the two totems of his guardian spirits coming together at one time. Taking a flint ax from his side, he scraped three cuts into his forearm: one to awaken him to this spiritual contact with his two most powerful guardians, the second to represent the claw of the bear, and the third to represent the talon of the eagle. These cuts symbolized his birth as a shaman.

The eagle swooped down on a school of partially submerged fish, grabbing the back of a fish with its talons. Removing the fish from the stream proved impossible, as it was too big to fly away with. The eagle walked the salmon to the stream bank. Watching carefully, the brave examined the eagle's use of its specialized claws. Out of respect, he waited for these guardian spirits, the masters of fishing, to finish feeding, while he whittled on a bone, sculpting a talon. Sharpening two more bones in like manner, he fastened the three to the end of a stick.

As the afternoon waned the bear's great appetite was satisfied, and the pile of stones representing each fish the bear had eaten had grown quite large. With a portion of fish, the eagle took flight towards a nest high in a tree. It was the brave's turn to fish the salmon stream. Still believing he was receiving a powerful gift on the edge of a dream, the man tried out his new discoveries.

First he entered the stream, chasing the fish towards the shore and then swatting a large salmon. The fish danced with energy. Unable to control it, the brave again swatted the fish up

towards the grass, still trying to grab it. With incredible strength, the fish continued its fight until the man found a rock and used it to end the battle. Rejoicing in pride, the man held the fish up to the sky. He tore a portion of the fish's flesh and ate it as the bear and eagle had. He left this first fish on the bank along with ornaments of roots, rocks and shells as gifts of honor to his mentors. After a few more successful attempts at catching fish by swatting them from the water, he decided to try out his new bone-stick. With some trial and error, he trapped a fish, but found himself unable to retrieve it. The bone stick would need some serrated edges to hook the fish. He realized his tool needed more work, so he pushed the stick through the gills of the fish he had already caught and carried them away.

Upon reaching a section of the river's eroded cliff, the sun began to set. The brave reflected on his gifts and the honor and experience of this day. He felt surrounded with strength, confidence, and skill. Like a bear, he was strong with new ways for survival. As the sun set along the bear trail, he saw the bear spirit once again and he felt the protection and power he gained from the bear. He knew the pride he would experience in returning with the gifts of fish and roots to his family and his delight in the stories he would relate that night around the fire.

Grand-Paw

(like a Bear out of Water)

THE SIZE AND WEIGHT OF A BEAR are difficult to assess. Distance only complicates this problem. When people see a bear close up, most will overestimate its size and weight. Any bear close up looks big! The vastness of the tundra can also throw off any calculation. When you see a bear far away on the tundra, it can be very difficult to guess its size, especially against a landscape that has only six-inch plants for scale. Brown bear males weigh 400 to 1,100 pounds, while brown bear females weigh 200 to 600 pounds. Adult brown bears average seven to nine feet in length. In comparison the largest bears, polar bears, measure eight to ten feet in length. Males weigh 600 to 1,200 pounds, with females weighing 400 to 700 pounds.

There is a bear at Alaska's Katmai National Park who is very well known, not only because he is huge, but because he has a peculiar feeding behavior with fish. As a young bear he was actually short and stout. He had difficulty accessing the prime fishing spots reserved by the more aggressive and larger bears. He was forced into the deep water away from the shallows and cascades where the salmon could be caught leaping. Left to his own resources, this bear developed a new strategy for fishing unique to bears of this area. He would dive underwater, completely disappearing, and stay under for 10, 20, or 30 seconds, surfacing with a fish more often than not. No other bears had been seen doing this—most bears generally dislike getting water in their ears. As a young bear, this one adapted to a niche not filled by other bears, and the local people gave him the nickname "Diver."

I didn't meet him until he was probably somewhere in his twenties. Fishermen who have been coming to Katmai since the late 1960s and early 1970s told me of seeing him around as a smaller bear back then. Some fishermen call him Scar Saddle after a large cross-shaped scar below his shoulder hump. My first contact was an impressive paw print on the beach near the campground. Not only was the print wide and long, it was pressed deeply into the sand. Thus the name Grand-Paw. It was in the fall when I first laid eyes on Grand-Paw—of course, he was eating an old dead salmon on the shoreline of the lake. The hair on his considerable belly took on the appearance of a flat-top haircut from constantly being dragged across the ground.

Grand-Paw prefers water to land transport. He seems slightly awkward on land; possibly his large size has begun to wear on his joints and limbs, perhaps a prior handicap has stiffened his mobility, or maybe he overheats on shore. On land, this big bear moves slowly, his weight shifting from side to side. In water he moves smoothly, gracefully, seemingly without effort.

Often he is found in the river asleep, with the back-half of his body still in the water and his "arms" holding onto the shore, fish-in-paw. If a hooligan occupies a fishing hole favored by human fishermen, complaints are sounded. But if Grand-Paw falls asleep on prime fishing territory, fishermen get lunch, clean fish, or nap themselves until he leaves. Grand-Paw's earned great respect and admiration. When friends know I've been to Katmai, before they ask how the trip was, they always ask if ol' Grand-Paw is still there.

Grand-Paw loves fish like no other bear. **No matter** what condition the fish is in, he will eat fresh or old with equal zeal. His weight has been guessed at one thousand pounds, nearly the upper limit for brown bears. I have watched Grand-Paw eat fish all day, nonstop. He often takes the last fish of his meal to a day bed, and placing the fish between his paws, he lies down to rest and snores away. I can imagine Grand-Paw dreaming about fish with his massive belly in a cool day-den he dug out along the shores of Naknek Lake. When he awakens after many twitching REM dreams about fish (or whatever bears dream about), a dead smelly fish awaits, no effort required. Watching bears for many years, I have never seen such a keen manner of pre-planning. Fresh and bright or mushy and green, no real preference in fish can be distinguished. Quantity is the menu choice for ol' Paw.

One fall night when we were camping in Katmai, Karen turned off the lantern and crawled into our tent. The hissing sound the lantern makes continued long after we snuggled ourselves into a sleeping bag. Karen unzipped the sleeping bag and tent and checked the lantern. To our surprise the lantern was indeed fully off. We both began to try to locate this strange sound wheezing away in the darkness, and to our surprise we found a massive hump of fur, just 10 feet away.

Knowing that this was our favorite bear made it a little less disturbing. After all, we were sure no other bear would come anywhere within the sound of his hissing and snoring. When he was young, Grand-Paw was small and easily bullied. Now, he doesn't move for anything or anyone. He was planted. We had no other choice; we went back to sleep. In the morning I watched as he arthritically rose and found some relief in the icy waters nearby, where he scrounged an old salmon off the bottom of the lake almost immediately.

Even though Grand-Paw is in his mid-twenties, he may have quite a life ahead. Bears are able to mate successfully after five or six years and then continue to have offspring in their teens and be a grandfather several times—in fact he probably is a great-Grand-Paw.

There is another large bear, probably in its late teens, that is as large as Grand-Paw with similar body and head proportions and characteristics. I call this bear "Son of a Bear." Son of a Bear is in his early- to mid-prime and is a paradigm of a coastal brown bear. Because of his size, physical likeness and fishing behavior, we originally named him Son of Grand-Paw. It's doubtful if their relatedness can be verified, but the possibility does exist in the imagination. The common thread between Grand-Paw and Son of a Bear is the time and energy they invest in catching fish.

Another bear-fish phenomenon is at Brooks Falls, Alaska, where the salmon practically leap into a waiting bear's mouth. At Brooks Falls, fish jump in a predictable path when following the stream upriver. Bears gravitate to a submerged rock that intersects the course taken by the salmon. If a bear stands on this prime location, fish will eventually jump where the bear can catch them with a turn of its neck. Many bears have adapted strategies specific to the rivers, streams, and lakes which they frequent. There are as many strategies as there are fishing locations, where adaptations develop depending on changes in water levels, the seasons, or the numbers of migrating salmon.

The number of fish and the time-energy equation ultimately affects the regional sizes of the bears. Some fish-eating black bears along the coast can be larger than interior grizzly bears of comparable ages. Black bears that can get as many fish as they want have grown to be quite large, reaching the upper size-limits of the species. Food plays a primary role in the morphological (size, shape, weight, and looks) characteristics of the bear.

Until recently, precise information about the age of bears in the wild was limited. In 1958, Will Troyer was working with the Kodiak National Wildlife Refuge. He tagged many bears, using a combination of a leg-hold snare, a galvanized bucket and a bottle of ether to anesthetize the bears. These were some of the first brown bears ever caught for research purposes. In 1991, a bear was shot by a hunter and examined by the Alaska Fish and Game. It had a numbered tag that Will had applied back in 1959. Troyer recalls that at the time of tagging it was around three or four years old, making it now about 35 years old. This was astounding news, as much to Will Troyer as it was to the whole scientific community.

Kennan Ward

A Bear Dance

in the Northern Lights

THE ATHABASCANS, THE NATIVE PEOPLE, called it "Denali" or the "Great One" out of respect. Maps call it Mount McKinley. On clear days you are able to see this great mountain from Fairbanks or from Anchorage and beyond, more than 100 miles away—although most of the time you can't see it even when you stand on its flanks. The 20,320-foot mountain builds its own weather pattern, masking itself from view the majority of the time.

My plan was to winter camp in search of northern lights, with the photographic backdrop of this magnificent mountain peak. Aside from a couple of winter ascents of the mountain, very few people actually camped in its wintery shadows, much less for three weeks or more. When Karen realized how cold it would be, she helped me to seek out a suitable partner for the trip. Everyone seemed interested, but nobody was ready to commit to the trip due to the cold. From mountaineering shops to outdoor gear manufacturers, everyone decided it was a nice idea, but not right for them.

Then a writer and conservationist friend, Glenn Stewart, decided to take leave of his wife and two children to travel with me and write a story about the northern lights. The first leg of our trip took us to Fairbanks; that first night was clear, so we went to a mountain called Murphy Dome to catch some luck. As we drove by a bank, its sign blinked a cool-of-the-night broadcast of downtown Fairbanks' time and temperature: 10 P.M., -27 degrees. Glenn and I had left our Idaho and California homes for a cold, new world.

The range of hills that surround Fairbanks funnels cold air to the bottom of the basin where the city is located. As we rose out of the bowl of Fairbanks it actually became warmer: my thermometer was reading in the minus-teens. That night the lights danced from the north to the east then to the zenith, shimmering curtains of green, white, and pink. With too many layers of clothes on to move, Glenn looked like a swollen monster in the reflection of the snow's light, but even with a monster's worth of clothes on we were cold. Standing around watching the night sky while exposing film to the beauty of the aurora meant we weren't moving around much, not enough to help the clothes do their job of keeping us warm.

It was exciting—the cold stimulated thoughts and ideas, deep philosophic explorations, thoughts that perhaps have inspired people for hundreds and thousands of years as they gazed up at the winter sky. Questions came to mind concerning how old the starlight was that we were viewing. How many people around countless campfires had viewed this same starlight? How many inspired ideas were formed while pondering the mystery of the night sky? The starlight shone down upon the earth, over all of her varying habitats, from ice-capped oceans to palm-adorned sandy beaches—we were up here in the far north enjoying the beauty of the aurora borealis, but wouldn't it be every bit as beautiful "down under" viewing the aurora australis?

The weather shifted and deteriorated; we began to miss the stars and the movement of the aurora. The next day was a typical Fairbanks inversion of warmth, cold, and fog. Our muscles hurt as if we had worked out or climbed a mountain; taut muscles are a typical response to cold-weather strain.

For the next five days bad weather kept us from getting out of town, let alone up onto Denali. Each evening we adjusted to nocturnal life and the cold, sometimes talking deep into the icy recesses of the night.

After a week of record snow and no outlook for clearing, Glenn decided the probability of his getting to the mountain was unlikely, particularly in light of his need to return to Idaho to his work of saving the wilderness lands. As time and weather became more of a factor we bade each other farewell: off he went to Idaho and off I went to wait for the weather to break in Talkeetna, the launching pad for climbs on Denali.

Two days later, a strange weather pattern developed in Talkeetna. There was a hazy fog and daytime temperatures were rising up into the teens. Cliff Hudson, a pioneer in the bush air-taxi business around the mountain, said it was a great day to fly. At 10 A.M. we packed the Super Cub—which seats one passenger behind the pilot—with some survival essentials and took off towards the mountain an hour or so away. The air temperature began to rise into the twenties as we traveled from 346 feet up to an air elevation of 2,000 feet along the Susitna River.

This route took us over glacial-carved wilderness accessible only by plane or an occasional dog sled or snowmobile. When we crossed the Tokositna River we were at an elevation of about 4,000 feet and the air temperature was in the thirties. Cliff tapped his thermometer in amazement upon reaching the Tokosha Mountains at 6,000 feet where the air temperature was—remarkably—in the mid-forties. We opened the windows for a photograph of the lateral moraines that stripe the glaciers and viewed a clearing air mass above our destination elevation near 7,000 feet.

As I scanned the glacier for possible photographs, I spotted a small patch of dirt on the otherwise pristine snow. Could the warm weather have triggered a bear to break out of its den? Hibernating bears in varying locations experience a 20 to 50 percent drop in metabolic rate. Some wake for a midwinter wander or change of den when a warm spell causes their dens to get damp. Though Cliff said there were no prior signs of bear denning at this elevation, I made him circle back several times—I'd waited for weeks at known den sites and never witnessed a bear's emergence. Sure enough there was a bear, digging by what must have been the entrance to its den. The sound of our plane made it disappear back inside, but I was satisfied. I had been dreaming of this for a long time: a rare exception to nature's norm that comes like a gift.

We explored further. Later that day we found our landing site. No one had landed there recently, because it was too early for the climbing season to have begun, so we braced for anything. We tried a couple of fly-by tests of the snow, and then down we went, sinking close to the belly of the fuselage. We donned snowshoes and still sank a foot or more in the dry, fluffy snow. We unloaded my gear and I viewed the glacier, my home for the next 20 days. We began to trample an area for the Super Cub to turn around and exit off the glacier.

Several hours were required for us to plod out a rough, snowy runway. At takeoff, with the engine running at near full I lifted the wing struts, first breaking free the frozen right ski, then over to the left side to break loose the left, then running back and forth pushing and lifting until finally the tail broke free and the small plane was moving! With a swerve the tail clipped me and sent me tumbling into the snow drift. On my knees, I turned to see the plane speeding down our makeshift runway, and the flying snow from the full-throttle engine blasted into my face, clogging my eyes and throat, leaving me unable to breathe for a few moments. Uncomfortable and without air, I passed an uncertain moment until I followed my instinct to swallow and clear the blocked air passage.

I regained my feet and saw the plane circle for a quick O.K. signal. Then the plane was gone and so was the sun, which dropped quickly below the horizon. I was clammy from the lift-off workout and the temperature had surely fallen 10 degrees with the setting sun. The 15 minutes of aircraft engine revving had sent snow drifts throughout the entire drop-off area, burying my gear. The darkness and chill stimulated immediate action—with ski poles I tested the soft snow and located my gear pile. Quickly I set up camp and prepared for a clear night, hopeful of northern lights.

Aurora Borealis

Close to the Arctic Circle during the midnight hours, northern lights move from horizon to zenith illuminating the sky with color. Somewhere on the night side of the earth, between the ionosphere and the semi-vacuum of outer space (5 to 50,000 miles away from the earth), electrons are accelerated to high speeds. Zooming along the curved pathway of the earth's magnetic field, they approach the earth's atmosphere at the poles. At altitudes of 50 to 200 miles these electrons collide with ions of hydrogen, nitrogen, and oxygen, exciting them to increased energy states. These particles quickly expel this new energy in the form of light—blue from hydrogen and nitrogen (positive) ions, red from neutral nitrogen, and dark red and light green from oxygen. The source point of the speeding electrons changes position, thus causing the colors to appear to wave across the sky. This awe-inspiring phenomenon is not completely understood, although prominent solar flares are followed by the most spectacular auroral displays.

From due north to due east a green arch developed over a period of three hours. About 1 A.M., when Ursa Major, the big bear or Big Dipper, was in the northeast sky, the arch broke towards the middle and began to move, rays of color pointing towards zenith. I was as excited as those ions in full collision. My camera batteries then failed from the -30 degree weather; my lens frosted and film cracked. With frustration I changed lenses and film and switched to totally manual operation as I saw the flare-up diminish. I was extremely disappointed that equipment failure had caused me to lose this opportunity. With all the preventative measures and thought put into the planning and preparation for this trip, I still was defeated by the harsh elements and the brutal cold.

The next few weeks were the quietest I have ever experienced: the deep cold and the natural beauty, mixed with the other-worldly phenomena of the aurora, created in me a philosophical, meditative state. Staring at the Big Dipper, Ursa Major, I clearly saw the large tail, body, head, and stance of the bear. With the Little Dipper, Ursa Minor, adjacent, the pair appeared as a mother and cub dancing through a sky aflame with color. I understood how aboriginal and modern-day people alike could imagine the bears as their spirits or guardians.

I had three weeks of icy seclusion, of life without trees, rocks, soil—nothing but snow-topped mountains all around. Alone on the breast of this glacier, reading these celestial messages in the dark heavens above me, was the closest I have come to understanding my own mysterious but real link with nature in a defining moment of time.

Selected Readings

Bledsoe, Thomas, *Brown Bear Summer: My Life Among Alaska's Grizzlies*, Penguin Books USA Inc.: New York, 1990.

Caras, Roger A., *Monarch of Deadman Bay: The Life and Death of a Kodiak Bear*, Bison Books: Lincoln, 1990.

Dufresne, Frank, *No Room For Bears: A Wilderness Writer's Experiences with a Threatened Breed*, Alaska Northwest Books: Anchorage, 1991.

Le Boeuf, Burney J., and Kaza, Stephanie, *The Natural History of Año Nuevo*, The Boxwood Press: Pacific Grove, 1981,

Lopez, Barry, *Arctic Dreams: Imagination and Desire in a Northern Landscape*, Bantam Books Inc.: New York, 1986.

Murie, Adolph, *The Grizzlies of Mount McKinley*, University of Washington Press: Seattle, 1987.

Walker, Tom, *River of Bears*, Voyageur Press: Stillwater, Minnesota, 1993.